Birds of New York

Field Guide
Second Edition

by Stan Tekiela

D0125830

Adventure Publications, Inc.
Cambridge, Minnesota

To my wife Katherine and daughter Abigail with all my love

Acknowledgments

Special thanks to the National Wildlife Refuge System, which stewards the land that is critical to many bird species. Thanks also to Dave Tetlow and Jeanne Skelly for reviewing the range maps.

Edited by Sandy Livoti and Deborah Walsh

Cover, book and CD design and illustrations by Jonathan Norberg

Range maps produced by Anthony Hertzel

Photo credits by photographer and page number:
Cover photo: Baltimore Oriole by Bill Marchel
Brian M. Collins: 232, 252 **Dudley Edmondson**: 72, 84, 90, 98 (female), 134 (both), 148 (soaring), 164 (both), 200, 202, 218 (perching, soaring), 264 (breeding), 272 (winter male), 28C **Kevin T. Karlson**: 36, 52 (juvenile), 118, 162 (female), 260 (winter), 276 (female), 28C **Bill Marchel:** 68 (male), 100 (white-striped), 104, 114, 130, 148 (perching), 242 **Maslowsk Wildlife Productions**: 22 (female), 74 (soaring), 86, 106, 176, 178, 194, 250, 282, 284 **Arthui Morris**: 52 (breeding) **Steve Mortensen**: 46, 96 (both), 156 **Warren Nelson**: 136 (female), 278 (female) **John Pennoyer**: 80 **Johann Schumacher/CLO***: 68 (female) **Brian E. Small**: 116 (winter), 120, 246 (yellow male), 262 (winter, juvenile), 264 (winter), 276 (male), 288 **Stan Tekiela**: 2, 4, 6 (both), 8, 10, 12, 14, 16 (both), 18 (perching, soaring), 20 (all), 22 (male), 24 (both), 26, 28 (both), 30 (both), 32 (both), 34 (both), 38, 40, 42, 44 (both), 48 (both), 50 (both), 54 (all), 56, 58 60, 62 (both), 64 (both), 66, 70, 74 (perching), 76, 78 (both), 82, 88, 92, 94, 98 (male), 100 (tan-striped), 102 (both), 108 (adult, 1 year old), 110, 112, 116 (breeding), 122 (female, juvenile), 124 126 (all), 128, 132, 136 (male), 138, 140 (both), 142, 144 (both), 146, 150 (both), 152, 154, 158 160, 162 (male), 166, 168 (soaring), 170 (male), 166, 170, 172 (both), 174, 180 (both), 182, 184 (all), 186, 188, 190, 192, 196, 198, 204, 206 (both), 208 (both), 210 (perching), 212, 214, 216 218 (juvenile), 222 (male, soaring), 224 (both), 226 (both), 228 (both), 230, 234, 236 (male, ir flight), 238, 240, 244, 246 (male), 248, 254 (male), 256, 258 (female, in flight), 260 (breeding, both in flight), 262 (breeding, in flight), 264 (juvenile), 266 (both), 268, 270, 272 (male, female), 274 (male), 278 (male), 290 (all), 292 **Brian K. Wheeler**: 18 (juvenile), 168 (female), 220 (all) **J. R. Woodward/CLO***: 210 (displaying) **Jim Zipp**: 108 (Bohemian), 274 (female)
*CLO: Cornell Laboratory of Ornithology

To the best of the publisher's knowledge, all photos were of live birds.

10 9 8 7
Copyright 2000, 2005 by Stan Tekiela
Published by Adventure Publications, Inc.
820 Cleveland Street South
Cambridge, MN 55008
1-800-678-7006
www.adventurepublications.net
All rights reserved
Printed in China
ISBN: 978-1-59193-108-9

TABLE OF CONTENTS

WHY WATCH BIRDS IN NEW YORK?

Millions of people have discovered bird feeding. It's a simple and enjoyable way to bring the beauty of birds closer to your home. Watching birds at your feeder and listening to them often leads to a lifetime pursuit of bird identification. The *Birds of New York Field Guide* is for those who want to identify the common birds of New York.

Listening to bird songs and learning about them is a wonderful way to expand your enjoyment of birds in New York. The optional *Birds of New York Audio CDs* contain nearly two hours of songs and calls of the birds in this book, as well as tips and mnemonics for learning the calls.

There are over 800 species of birds found in North America. In New York alone there have been more than 450 kinds of birds recorded through the years. These bird sightings were diligently recorded by hundreds of bird watchers and became part of the official state record. From these records, I've chosen 120 of the most common and easily seen birds of New York to include in this field guide.

Bird watching, often called birding, is the largest spectator sport in America. Its outstanding popularity in New York is due, in part, to an unusually rich and abundant birdlife. Why are there so many birds? One reason is open space. New York is over 49,000 square miles (127,400 sq. km), making it the thirtieth largest state. Despite its large size, only a little over 18.3 million people call New York home. On average, that is 373 people per square mile (144 per sq. km), half of whom live in and around New York City.

Open space is not the only reason there is such an abundance of birds–it's also the diversity of habitat. From the windswept shores of the Atlantic Ocean to the top of the Adirondack and Catskill Mountains and on to the shores of Lake Ontario, New York is rich in natural habitat that is perfect for birds.

The state can be broken into many distinctly different habitats, each of which supports a different group of birds. Long-legged shorebirds such as Sanderlings gravitate to beaches along the Atlantic, while tiny, brightly colored warblers such as American Redstarts flit from tree to tree in New York's northern forests.

Another great feature in northern New York is the Adirondack Mountains. A beautiful range of hills and rounded peaks, the Adirondacks are covered with coniferous forests with Balsam Firs and White Pines. This is an area where you can find birds such as Brown Creepers and Purple Finches.

In southern and central parts of New York, oaks and maples in deciduous forests are home to birds such as Scarlet Tanagers and Great Crested Flycatchers.

A low area in the northwestern portion of New York known as the Great Lakes Plain is essentially a flat region having little to no relief. This flat open space is mostly agricultural, but still provides good habitat for birds in large flocks such as Horned Larks.

Western New York borders on two of the Great Lakes—Lake Erie and Lake Ontario. These large freshwater lakes are home to many species of birds such as Herring and Ring-billed Gulls.

Besides its varying habitats, New York is known for its weather extremes. From the snowy winters in the northwestern part of the state to the steamy summers in the south, seasonal changes accompany a changing array of birds.

No matter where you are in the state, there are birds to watch in every season. Whether witnessing a migration of hawks in the fall or welcoming back the hummingbirds in spring, there is variety and excitement in birding in New York as each season turns to the next.

OBSERVE WITH A STRATEGY; TIPS FOR IDENTIFYING BIRDS

Identifying birds isn't as difficult as you might think. By simply following a few basic strategies, you can increase your chances of successfully identifying most birds you see! One of the first and easiest things to do when you see a new bird is to note its color. (Also, since this book is organized by color, you will go right to that color section to find it.)

Next, note the size of the bird. A strategy to quickly estimate size is to select a small-, medium- and large-sized bird to use for reference. For example, most people are familiar with robins. A robin, measured from tip of the bill to tip of the tail, is 10 inches (25 cm) long. Using the robin as an example of a medium-sized bird, select two other birds, one smaller and one larger. Many people use a House Sparrow, at about 6 inches (15 cm), and an American Crow, about 18 inches (45 cm). When you see a bird that you don't know, you can quickly ask yourself, "Is it smaller than a robin, but larger than a sparrow?" When you look in your field guide to help identify your bird, you'll know it is roughly between 6-10 inches (15-25 cm) long. This will help to narrow your choices.

Next, note the size, shape and color of the bill. Is it long, short, thick, thin, pointed, blunt, curved or straight? Seed-eating birds such as Northern Cardinals have bills that are thick and strong enough to crack even the toughest seeds. Birds that sip nectar such as Ruby-throated Hummingbirds need long thin bills to reach deep into flowers. Hawks and owls tear their prey with very sharp, curving bills. Sometimes, just noting the bill shape can help you decide whether the bird is a woodpecker, sparrow, grosbeak, blackbird or bird of prey.

Next, take a look around and note the habitat in which you see the bird. Is it wading in a saltwater marsh? Walking along a riverbank or on the beach? Soaring in the sky? Is it perched high in the trees or hopping along the forest floor? Because of

their preferences in diet and habitat, you will usually see robins hopping on the ground, but not often eating seeds at a feeder. Or you might see a Blue Jay sitting on the branches of a tree, but not climbing headfirst down a tree trunk like a White-breasted Nuthatch.

Noticing what a bird is eating will give you another clue to help you identify that bird. Feeding is a big part of any bird's life. Fully one-third of all bird activity revolves around searching for and catching food, or actually eating. While birds don't always follow all the rules of what we think they eat, you can make some general assumptions. Northern Flickers, for instance, feed upon ants and other insects, so you wouldn't expect to see them visiting a backyard feeder. Some birds such as Barn Swallows and Tree Swallows feed upon flying insects and spend hours swooping and diving to catch a meal.

Sometimes you can identify a bird by the way it perches. Body posture can help you differentiate between an American Crow and a Red-tailed Hawk. American Crows lean forward over their feet on a branch, while hawks perch in a vertical position. Look for this the next time you see a large unidentified bird in a tree.

Birds in flight are often difficult to identify, but noting the size and shape of the wing will help. A bird's wing size is in direct proportion to its body size, weight and type of flying. The shape of the wing determines if the bird flies fast and with precision, or slowly and less precisely. Birds such as House Finches, which flit around in thick tangles of branches, have short round wings. Birds that soar on warm updrafts of air, such as Turkey Vultures, have long broad wings. Barn Swallows have short pointed wings that slice through the air, propelling their swift and accurate flight.

Some birds have unique patterns of flight that aid in identification. American Goldfinches fly in a distinctive up-and-down pattern that makes it look as if they are riding a roller coaster.

While it's not easy to make these observations in the short time you often have to watch a "mystery bird," practicing these methods of identification will greatly expand your skills in birding. Also, seek the guidance of a more experienced birder who will help you improve your skills and answer questions on the spot.

Bird Songs and Calls

Another part of bird identification involves using your ears. A song or call can be enough to positively identify a bird without seeing it. If you see a bird that you don't know, the song or call can help you identify it. To learn about bird songs, calls, how they are produced, what they mean and how they are used, see the companion *Birds of New York Audio CDs*.

BIRD BASICS

It's easier to identify birds and communicate about them if you know the names of the different parts of a bird. For instance, it's more effective to use the word "crest" to indicate the set of extra long feathers on top of a Northern Cardinal's head than to try to describe it.

The following illustration points out the basic parts of a bird. Because it is a composite of many birds, it shouldn't be confused with any actual bird.

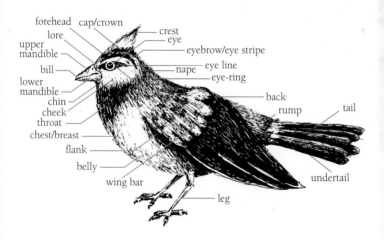

Bird Color Variables

No other animal has a color palette like a bird's. Brilliant blues, lemon yellows, showy reds and iridescent greens are common-place within the bird world. In general, the male birds are more colorful than their female counterparts. This is probably to help the male attract a mate, essentially saying, "Hey, look at me!" It also calls attention to the male's overall health. The better the condition of his feathers, the better his food source and territory, and therefore the better his potential for a mate.

Female birds that don't look like their male counterparts (such species are called sexually dimorphic, meaning "two forms") are often a nondescript color, as seen with the Indigo Bunting. These muted tones help hide the females during weeks of motionless incubation, and draw less attention to them when they are out feeding or taking a break from the rigors of raising their young.

In some species such as the Bald Eagle, Blue Jay and Downy Woodpecker, male birds look nearly identical to the females. In the case of woodpeckers, the sexes are differentiated by only a single red mark or sometimes a yellow mark. Depending upon the species, the mark may be on top of the head, face, nape of neck or just behind the bill.

During the first year, juvenile birds often look like the mothers. Since brightly colored feathers are used mainly for attracting a mate, young non-breeding males don't have a need for colorful plumage. It is not until the first spring molt (or several years later, depending on the species) that young males obtain their breeding colors.

Both breeding and winter plumages are the result of molting. Molting is the process of dropping old worn feathers and replacing them with new ones. All birds molt, typically twice a year, with the spring molt usually occurring in late winter. During this time, most birds produce their breeding plumage (brighter colors for attracting mates), which lasts throughout the summer.

Winter plumage is the result of the late summer molt, which serves a couple of important functions. First, it adds feathers for warmth in the coming winter season. Second, in some species it produces feathers that tend to be drab in color, which helps to camouflage the birds and hide them from predators. The winter plumage of the male American Goldfinch, for example, is olive brown unlike its obvious canary yellow color during summer. Luckily for us, some birds such as the male Northern Cardinal retain their bright summer colors all year long.

Bird Nests

Bird nests are truly an amazing feat of engineering. Imagine building your home strong enough to weather a storm, large enough to hold your entire family, insulated enough to shelter them from cold and heat, and waterproof enough to keep out rain. Now, build it without any blueprints or directions, and without the use of your hands or feet! Birds do!

Before building a nest, an appropriate site must be selected. In some species such as House Wrens, the male picks out several potential sites and assembles several small twigs in each. This discourages other birds from using nearby nest cavities. These "extra" nests are occasionally called dummy nests. The female is then taken around and shown all the choices. She chooses her favorite and finishes constructing the nest. In some other species of birds–Baltimore Orioles, for example–it is the female who chooses the site and constructs the nest, with the male offering only an occasional suggestion. Each species has its own nest-building routine, which is strictly followed.

As you'll see in the following illustrations, birds build a wide variety of nest types.

ground nest   **platform nest**   **cup nest**   **pendulous nest**   **cavity nest**

Nesting material often consists of natural elements found in the immediate area. Most nests consist of plant fibers (such as bark peeled from grapevines), sticks, mud, dried grass, feathers, fur, or soft fuzzy tufts from thistle. Some birds, including Ruby-throated Hummingbirds, use spider webs to glue nest materials together. Nesting material is limited to what a bird can hold or carry. Because of this, a bird must make many trips afield to gather enough materials to complete its nest. Most nests take at least four days or more, and hundreds, if not thousands, of trips to build.

The simple **ground nest** is scraped out of the earth. A shallow depression that usually contains no nesting material, it is made by birds such as the Killdeer and Horned Lark.

Another kind of nest, the **platform nest**, represents a more complex type of nest building. Constructed of small twigs and branches, the platform nest is a simple arrangement of sticks which forms a platform and features a small depression to nestle the eggs.

Some platform nests, such as those of the Canada Goose, are constructed on the ground and are made with mud and grass. Platform nests can also be on cliffs, bridges, balconies or even in flowerpots. This kind of nest gives space to adventurous youngsters and functions as a landing platform for the parents. Many waterfowl build platform nests on the ground, usually near water or actually in water. These floating platform nests vary with the water level, thus preventing nests with eggs from being flooded. Platform nests, constructed by such birds as Mourning Doves and herons, are not anchored to the tree and may tumble from the branches during high winds and storms.

The **cup nest** is a modified platform nest, used by three-quarters of all songbirds. Constructed from the outside in, a supporting platform is constructed first. This platform is attached firmly to a tree, shrub, rock ledge or the ground. Next, the sides are constructed of grasses, small twigs, bark or leaves, which are woven together and often glued with mud for added strength. The inner cup, lined with feathers, animal fur, soft plant material or animal hair, is constructed last. The mother bird uses her chest to cast the final contours of the inner nest.

The **pendulous nest** is an unusual nest, looking more like a sock hanging from a branch than a nest. Inaccessible to most predators, these nests are attached to the ends of the smallest branches of a tree and often wave wildly in the breeze. Woven very tightly of plant fibers, they are strong, watertight and take up to a week to construct. More commonly used by tropical birds, this complicated type of nest has also been mastered by orioles and kinglets. A small opening on the top or side allows the parents access to the grass-lined interior. (It must be one heck of a ride to be inside one of these nests during a windy spring thunderstorm!)

Another type of nest, the **cavity nest**, is used by many bird species, including woodpeckers and Eastern Bluebirds. The cavity nest is usually excavated in a tree branch or trunk and offers shelter from storms, sun, predators and cold. A relatively small entrance hole in a tree leads to an inner chamber up to 10 inches (25 cm) below. Usually constructed by woodpeckers, the cavity nest is typically used only once by its builder, but subsequently can be used for many years by birds such as Tree Swallows, mergansers and bluebirds, which do not have the capability of excavating one for themselves. Kingfishers, on the other hand, excavate a tunnel up to 4 feet (1 m) long, which connects the entrance in a riverbank to the nest chamber. These cavity nests are often sparsely lined because they are already well insulated.

Some birds, including some swallows, take nest building one step further. They use a collection of small balls of mud to construct an adobe-style home. Constructed beneath the eaves of houses, under bridges or inside chimneys, some of these nests look like simple cup nests. Others are completely enclosed, with small tunnel-like openings that lead into a safe nesting chamber for the baby birds.

One of the most clever of all nest types is known as the **no nest** or daycare nest. Parasitic birds such as Brown-headed Cowbirds build no nests at all! The egg-laden female expertly searches out other birds' nests and sneaks in to lay one of her own eggs while the host mother is not looking, thereby leaving the host mother to raise an adopted youngster. The mother cowbird wastes no energy building a nest only to have it raided by a predator. By using several nests of other birds, she spreads out her progeny so at least one of her offspring will live to maturity.

Who Builds the Nest?

In general, the female bird builds the nest. She gathers nesting materials and constructs a nest, with an occasional visit from her mate to check on progress. In some species, both parents contribute equally to the construction of a nest. A male bird might forage for precisely the right sticks, grass or mud, but it is often the female that forms or puts together the nest. She uses her body to form the egg chamber. Rarely does the male build a nest by himself.

Fledging

Fledging is the interval between hatching and flight or leaving the nest. Some birds leave the nest within hours of hatching (precocial), but it might be weeks before they are able to fly. This is common with waterfowl and shorebirds. Until they start to fly, they are called fledglings. Birds that are still in the nest are called nestlings. Other baby birds are born naked and blind, and remain in the nest for several weeks (altricial).

Why Birds Migrate

Why do birds migrate? The short answer is simple—food. Birds migrate to areas with high concentrations of food, as it is easier to breed where food is than where it is not. A typical migrating bird—the Scarlet Tanager, for instance—will migrate from the tropics of Central and South America to nest in forests of North America, taking advantage of billions of newly hatched insects to feed its young. This trip is called **complete migration**.

Some birds of prey return from their complete migration to northern regions that are overflowing with small rodents such as mice and voles that have continued to breed in winter.

Complete migrators have a set time and pattern of migration. Each year at nearly the same time, they take off and head for a specific wintering ground. Complete migrators may travel great distances, sometimes as much as 15,000 miles (24,150 km) or more in one year. But complete migration does not necessarily imply flying from the frozen northland to a tropical destination. The Dark-eyed Junco, for example, is a complete migrator that flies from the far reaches of Canada to spend the winter right here in New York. This is still called complete migration.

There are many interesting aspects to complete migrators. In the spring, males usually migrate several weeks before the females, arriving early to scope out possibilities for nesting sites and food sources, and to begin to defend territories. The females arrive several weeks later. In the autumn, in many species, the females and their young leave early, often up to four weeks before the adult males.

All migrators are not the same type. **Partial migrators** such as American Goldfinches usually wait until food supplies dwindle before flying south. Unlike complete migrators, partial migrators move only far enough south, or sometimes east and west, to find abundant food. In some years it might be only a few hundred miles, while in other years it might be nearly a thousand. This kind of migration, dependent on weather and the availability of food, is sometimes called seasonal movement.

Unlike the predictable ebbing and flowing behavior of complete migrators or partial migrators, **irruptive migrators** can move every third to fifth year or, in some cases, in consecutive years. These migrations are triggered when times are really tough and food is scarce. Purple Finches are a good example of irruptive migrators, because they leave their normal northern range in search of food or in response to overpopulation.

How Do Birds Migrate?

One of the many secrets of migration is fat. While we humans are fighting the battle of the bulge, birds intentionally gorge themselves to put on as much fat as possible while still being able to fly. Fat provides the greatest amount of energy per unit of weight, and in the same way that your car needs gas, birds are propelled by fat and stalled without it.

During long migratory flights, fat deposits are used up quickly, and birds need to stop to "refuel." This is when backyard bird feeding stations and undeveloped, natural spaces around our towns and cities are especially important. Some birds require up to 2-3 days of constant feeding to build their fat reserves before continuing their seasonal trip.

Some birds such as most eagles, hawks, ospreys, falcons and vultures migrate during the day. Larger birds can hold more body fat, go longer without eating and take longer to migrate. These birds glide along on rising columns of warm air, called thermals, which hold them aloft while they slowly make their way north or south. They generally rest during the night and hunt early in the morning before the sun has a chance to warm the land and create good soaring conditions. Birds migrating during the day use a combination of landforms, rivers, and the rising and setting sun to guide them in the right direction.

Most other birds migrate during the night. Studies show that some birds which migrate at night use the stars to navigate. Others use the setting sun, while still others such as doves use the earth's magnetic fields to guide them north or south. While flying at night might seem like a crazy idea, nocturnal migration is safer for several reasons. First, there are fewer nighttime predators for migrating birds. Second, traveling at night allows time during the day to find food in unfamiliar surroundings. Finally, nighttime wind patterns tend to be flat, or laminar. These flat winds don't have the turbulence associated with daytime winds and can actually help carry smaller birds by pushing them along.

HOW TO USE THIS GUIDE

To help you quickly and easily identify birds, this field guide is organized by color. Simply note the color of the bird and turn to that section. Refer to the first page for the color key. The Red-headed Woodpecker, for example, is black and white with a red head. Because this bird is mostly black and white, it will be found in the black and white section. Each color section is also arranged by size, generally with the smaller birds first. Sections may also incorporate the average size in a range, which, in some cases, reflects size differences between male and female birds. Flip through the pages in that color section to find the bird. If you already know the name of the bird, check the index for the page number. In some species, the male and female are remarkably different in color. In others, the color of breeding and winter plumages differs. These species will have an inset photograph with a page reference and in most cases are found in two color sections.

In the description section you will find a variety of information about the bird. On page 1 is a sample of information included in the book.

Range Maps

Range maps are included for each bird. Colored areas indicate where in New York a particular bird is most likely to be found. The colors represent the presence of a species during a specific season, not the density or amount of birds in the area. Green is used for summer, blue for winter, red for year-round and yellow for areas where the bird is seen during migration. While every effort has been made to accurately depict these ranges, they are only general guidelines. Ranges actually change on an ongoing basis due to a variety of factors. Changes in the weather, species abundance, landscape and vital resources such as availability of food and water can affect local populations, migration and movements, causing birds to be found in areas that are atypical for the species.

Colored areas simply mean bird sightings for that species have been frequent in those areas and less frequent in others. Please use the maps as intended–as general guides only.

Using the Companion *Birds of New York Audio CDs*

The CD icon at the bottom of each description page includes a track number for the bird on the *Birds of New York Audio CDs*. Play the track number to hear the bird's songs and calls. Bird songs and calls on the CDs are organized in the same order as the birds in the book. For species in which the male and female are different colors (sexually dimorphic) or when the breeding and winter plumage color differs, the birds are shown in the book in two color sections. On the CDs the recording of a species is presented only once and coincides with the first time the bird is shown in the book.

Common Name

Scientific name

YEAR-ROUND
MIGRATION
SUMMER
WINTER

Size: measures head to tail, may include wingspan

Male: a brief description of the male bird, and may include breeding, winter or other plumages

Female: a brief description of the female bird, which is sometimes not the same as the male

Juvenile: a brief description of the juvenile bird, which often looks like the female

Nest: the kind of nest this bird builds to raise its young; who builds the nest; how many broods per year

Eggs: how many eggs you might expect to see in a nest; color and marking

Incubation: the average time parents spend incubating the eggs; who does the incubation

Fledging: the average time young spend in the nest after hatching but before they leave the nest; who does the most "childcare" and feeding

Migration: complete (consistent, seasonal), partial (seasonal movement, destination varies), irruptive (unpredictable, depends on the food supply), non-migrator; additional comments

Food: what the bird eats most of the time (e.g., seeds, insects, fruit, nectar, small mammals, fish); if it typically comes to a bird feeding station

Compare: notes about other birds that look similar and the pages on which they can be found, may include extra information to help identify

Stan's Notes: Interesting gee-whiz natural history information. This could be something to look or listen for, or something to help positively identify the bird. Also includes remarkable features.

Track number on *Birds of New York Audio CDs* (sold separately). 1

female
pg. 107

male

Eastern Towhee
Pipilo erythrophthalmus

YEAR-ROUND SUMMER

Size: 7-8" (18-20 cm)

Male: A mostly black bird with dirty red brown sides and a white belly. Long black tail with white tip. Short, stout, pointed bill and rich red eyes. White wing patches flash in flight.

Female: similar to male, but is brown, not black

Juvenile: light brown, a heavily streaked head, chest and belly, long dark tail with white tip

Nest: cup; female builds; 2 broods per year

Eggs: 3-4; creamy white with brown markings

Incubation: 12-13 days; female incubates

Fledging: 10-12 days; male and female feed young

Migration: complete, to southern states, Mexico and Central and South America

Food: insects, seeds, fruit; visits ground feeders

Compare: Slightly smaller than the American Robin (pg. 209), which lacks the white belly. The Gray Catbird (pg. 205) lacks the black head and rusty sides. Common Grackle (pg. 11) lacks a white belly and has a long thin bill. Male Rose-breasted Grosbeak (pg. 27) has a rosy patch in the center of its chest.

Stan's Notes: Common name comes from its distinctive "tow-hee" call given by both sexes. Mostly known for its characteristic call that sounds like, "Drink-your-tea!" Seen hopping backward with both feet (bilateral scratching), raking up leaf litter for insects and seeds. The female broods, but male does the most feeding of young. In southern coastal states, some have red eyes; others have white eyes.

female
pg. 111

male

Brown-headed Cowbird
Molothrus ater

Size: 7½" (19 cm)

Male: A glossy black bird, reminiscent of the Red-winged Blackbird. Chocolate brown head with a pointed, sharp gray bill.

Female: dull brown bird with bill similar to male

Juvenile: similar to female, only dull gray color and a streaked chest

Nest: no nest; lays eggs in nests of other birds

Eggs: 5-7; white with brown markings

Incubation: 10-13 days; host bird incubates eggs

Fledging: 10-11 days; host birds feed young

Migration: non-migrator in New York

Food: insects, seeds; will come to seed feeders

Compare: The male Red-winged Blackbird (pg. 9) is slightly larger with red and yellow patches on upper wings. Common Grackle (pg. 11) has a long tail and lacks the brown head. European Starling (pg. 7) has a shorter tail.

Stan's Notes: A member of the blackbird family. Of approximately 750 species of parasitic birds worldwide, this is the only parasitic bird in New York, laying eggs in host birds' nests, leaving others to raise its young. Cowbirds are known to have laid eggs in nests of over 200 species of birds. Some birds reject cowbird eggs, but most incubate them and raise the young, even to the exclusion of their own. Look for warblers and other birds feeding young birds twice their own size. At one time cowbirds followed bison to feed on insects attracted to the animals.

winter

breeding

European Starling
Sturnus vulgaris

YEAR-ROUND

Size: 7½" (19 cm)

Male: Gray-to-black bird with white speckles in fall and winter. Shiny purple black during spring and summer. Long, pointed yellow bill in spring turns gray in fall. Short tail.

Female: same as male

Juvenile: similar to adult, gray brown in color with a streaked chest

Nest: cavity; male and female line cavity; 2 broods per year

Eggs: 4-6; bluish with brown markings

Incubation: 12-14 days; female and male incubate

Fledging: 18-20 days; female and male feed young

Migration: non-migrator to partial; will move around to find food

Food: insects, seeds, fruit; comes to seed and suet feeders

Compare: Similar to Common Grackle (pg. 11), but lacks its long tail. The male Brown-headed Cowbird (pg. 5) is the same size, but has a brown head and longer tail.

Stan's Notes: A great songster, this bird can mimic other birds and sounds. Often displaces woodpeckers, chickadees and other cavity-nesting birds. Can be very aggressive and destroy eggs or young of other birds. Bill changes color with the seasons: yellow in spring, gray in autumn. Jaws are designed to be the most powerful when opening, as they pry open crevices to locate hidden insects. Gathers in the hundreds in autumn. Not a native bird, it was introduced to New York City in 1890-91 from Europe.

female pg. 125

male

YEAR-ROUND

Red-winged Blackbird
Agelaius phoeniceus

Size: 8½" (22 cm)

Male: Jet black bird with red and yellow shoulder patches on upper wings. Pointed black bill.

Female: heavily streaked brown bird with a pointed brown bill and white eyebrows

Juvenile: same as female

Nest: cup; female builds; 2-3 broods per year

Eggs: 3-4; bluish green with brown markings

Incubation: 10-12 days; female incubates

Fledging: 11-14 days; female and male feed young

Migration: partial to non-migrator in New York

Food: seeds, insects; will come to seed feeders

Compare: Slightly larger than the male Brown-headed Cowbird (pg. 5), but is less iridescent and lacks the Cowbird's brown head. Differs from all other blackbirds due to the red and yellow patches on its wings (epaulets).

Stan's Notes: One of the most widespread and numerous birds in New York. It is a sure sign of spring when Red-winged Blackbirds return to the marshes. Flocks of up to 100,000 birds have been reported. Males return before the females and defend territories by singing from tops of surrounding vegetation. Males repeat call from the tops of cattails while showing off their red and yellow wing bars (epaulets). Females choose a mate and will often nest over shallow water in thick stands of cattails. Red-wingeds feed mostly on seeds in fall and spring, switching to insects during summer.

YEAR-ROUND
SUMMER

Common Grackle
Quiscalus quiscula

Size: 11-13" (28-33 cm)

Male: Large black bird with iridescent blue black head, purple brown body, long black tail, long thin bill and bright golden eyes.

Female: similar to male, only duller and smaller

Juvenile: similar to female

Nest: cup; female builds; 2 broods per year

Eggs: 4-5; greenish white with brown markings

Incubation: 13-14 days; female incubates

Fledging: 16-20 days; female and male feed young

Migration: complete, to southern states, non-migrator in Long Island

Food: fruit, seeds, insects; comes to seed feeders

Compare: European Starling (pg. 7) is much smaller with a speckled appearance, and yellow bill during the breeding season. The male Red-winged Blackbird (pg. 9) has red and yellow wing markings.

Stan's Notes: Usually nests in small colonies of up to 75 pairs, but travels with other blackbirds in large flocks. Is known to feed in farmers' fields. Male holds tail in a vertical keel-like position during flight. The flight pattern is almost always level, as opposed to an undulating up-and-down movement. Unlike most birds, it has larger muscles for opening the mouth (rather than for closing it) and prying crevices apart to locate hidden insects. The name is derived from the Latin word *graculus*, meaning "to cough," for its loud raspy call.

CD 1, TRACK 6

11

American Coot
Fulica americana

Size: 13-16" (33-40 cm)

Male: Slate gray to black all over. White bill with a dark band near tip. Green legs and feet. A small white patch near the base of the tail. Prominent red eyes. Small red patch above bill between eyes.

Female: same as male

Juvenile: much paler than adult, with a gray bill and same white rump patch

Nest: cup; female and male build; 1 brood per year

Eggs: 9-12; pinkish buff with brown markings

Incubation: 21-25 days; female and male incubate

Fledging: 49-52 days; female and male feed young

Migration: complete, to southern states, Mexico and Central America

Food: insects, aquatic plants

Compare: Smaller than most other waterfowl. This is the only black water bird or duck-like bird with a white bill.

Stan's Notes: An excellent diver and swimmer, often seen in large flocks on open water. Not a duck, as it has large lobed toes instead of webbed feet. When taking off, scrambles across surface of water with wings flapping. Bobs head while swimming. Floating nests are anchored to vegetation. Huge flocks of as many as 1,000 birds gather for migration. The unusual common name "Coot" is of unknown origin, but in Middle English, *coote* was used to describe various waterfowl–perhaps it stuck. Also called Mud Hen.

American Crow
Corvus brachyrhynchos

Size: 18" (45 cm)

Male: All-black bird with black bill, legs and feet. Can have a purple sheen in direct sunlight.

Female: same as male

Juvenile: same as adult

Nest: platform; female builds; 1 brood per year

Eggs: 4-6; bluish to olive green with brown marks

Incubation: 18 days; female incubates

Fledging: 28-35 days; female and male feed young

Migration: non-migrator to partial

Food: fruit, insects, mammals, fish, carrion; will come to seed and suet feeders

Compare: Similar to the Common Raven (pg. 17), but has a smaller bill and lacks shaggy throat feathers. The American Crow has a higher-pitched call than deep, low raspy call of the Common Raven. The American Crow has a squared tail. Common Raven has a wedge-shaped tail, apparent in flight.

Stan's Notes: One of the most recognizable birds in New York. Often reuses its nest every year if not taken over by a Great Horned Owl. Collects and stores bright, shiny objects in the nest. Able to mimic other birds and human voices. One of the smartest of all birds and very social, often entertaining itself by provoking chases with other birds. Feeds on road kill but is rarely hit by cars. Can live up to 20 years. Unmated birds known as helpers help raise the young. Large extended families roost together at night, dispersing during the day to hunt.

 CD 1, TRACK 8

in flight

Common Raven
Corvus corax

Size: 22-27" (56-69 cm)

Male: Large all-black bird with a large black bill, a shaggy beard of feathers on the chin and throat, and a large wedge-shaped tail, seen in flight.

Female: same as male

Juvenile: same as adult

Nest: platform; female and male build; 1 brood per year

Eggs: 4-6; pale green with brown markings

Incubation: 18-21 days; female incubates

Fledging: 38-44 days; female and male feed young

Migration: non-migrator to partial

Food: insects, fruit, small animals, carrion

Compare: Larger than its cousin, the American Crow (pg. 15), which lacks the throat patch of feathers. Glides on flat, outstretched wings unlike the slightly V-shaped pattern of the Crow. Low, raspy call distinguishes Raven from the higher-pitched Crow.

Stan's Notes: This bird is a symbol of New York's northern woods. Considered by some to be the smartest of all birds. Known for its aerial acrobatics and long swooping dives. Scavenges with crows and gulls. Known to follow wolf packs around to pick up scraps and pick at bones of a kill. Complex courtship includes grabbing bills, preening each other and cooing. Most begin to breed at 3-4 years of age. Mates for life. Uses the same nest site for many years.

soaring

juvenile

SUMMER

Turkey Vulture
Cathartes aura

Size: 26-32" (66-80 cm); up to 6-foot wingspan

Male: Large bird with obvious red head and legs. In flight, the wings appear two-toned: black leading edge with gray on the trailing edge and tip. The tips of wings end in finger-like projections. Long squared tail. Ivory bill.

Female: same as male

Juvenile: similar to adult, with gray-to-blackish head and bill

Nest: no nest, or minimal nest on cliff or in cave; 1 brood per year

Eggs: 2; white with brown markings

Incubation: 38-41 days; female and male incubate

Fledging: 66-88 days; female and male feed young

Migration: complete, to southern states, Mexico and Central and South America

Food: carrion; parents regurgitate for young

Compare: Smaller than the Bald Eagle (pg. 55), look for Turkey Vulture's two-toned wings. Flies holding wings in a slight V shape unlike the Bald Eagle's straight wing position.

Stan's Notes: The vulture's naked head is an adaptation to reduce risk of feather fouling (picking up diseases) from carcasses. Unlike hawks and eagles, it has weak feet more suited to walking than grasping. One of the few birds that has a developed sense of smell. Mostly mute, making only grunts and groans. Seen in trees with wings outstretched, sunning itself. Recent studies show this bird is closely related to storks, not birds of prey.

MUTE (not on CD)

in flight

juvenile

crests

drying

Double-crested Cormorant
Phalacrocorax auritus

MIGRATION
SUMMER

Size: 33" (84 cm)

Male: Large black water bird with a long snake-like neck. Two crests on head. Long gray bill with yellow at the base and a hooked tip.

Female: same as male

Juvenile: lighter brown with a grayish chest and neck

Nest: platform, in colony; male and female build; 1 brood per year

Eggs: 3-4; bluish white without markings

Incubation: 25-29 days; female and male incubate

Fledging: 37-42 days; male and female feed young

Migration: complete, to southern states, Mexico and Central America

Food: small fish, aquatic insects

Compare: Similar size as the Turkey Vulture (pg. 19), which also perches on branches with wings open to dry in the sun, but Turkey Vulture has a naked red head. Twice the size of the American Coot (pg. 13), which lacks the Cormorant's long neck and bill.

Stan's Notes: Often seen flying in large V formation. Usually roosts in large groups in trees close to water. Catches fish by swimming underwater with wings held at its sides. Lacks the oil gland that keeps feathers from becoming waterlogged. To dry off it strikes an erect pose with wings outstretched, facing the sun. Common name refers to the two crests on its head, which are not usually seen. "Cormorant" comes from the Latin *corvus*, meaning "crow," and *L. marinus*, meaning "pertaining to the sea," literally, "Sea Crow."

male

female

Black-and-white Warbler
Mniotilta varia

MIGRATION
SUMMER

Size: 5" (13 cm)

Male: Striped like a zebra, this small warbler has a distinctive black-and-white striped cap. White belly. Black chin and cheek patch.

Female: same as male, only duller and without the black chin and cheek patch

Juvenile: similar to female

Nest: cup; female builds; 1 brood per year

Eggs: 4-5; white with brown markings

Incubation: 10-11 days; female incubates

Fledging: 9-12 days; female and male feed young

Migration: complete, to Florida, Mexico, Central and South America

Food: insects

Compare: Look for Black-and-white Warbler to creep down tree trunks headfirst, like the Red-breasted and White-breasted Nuthatches (pp. 181 and 189, respectively).

Stan's Notes: The only warbler that moves headfirst down a tree trunk. Look for this common warbler searching for insect eggs in the bark of large trees. Song sounds like a slowly turning, squeaky wheel. Female will perform a distraction dance to draw predators away from the nest. Makes its nest on the ground, concealed under dead leaves or at the base of a tree. One of the first warblers to return in spring. Common summer resident in the state, although more conspicuous during migration. Most arrive in April and May and leave by September.

male

female

Downy Woodpecker
Picoides pubescens

YEAR-ROUND

Size: 6" (15 cm)

Male: A small woodpecker with an all-white belly, black-and-white spotted wings, a black line running through the eyes, a short black bill, a white stripe down the back and red mark on the back of the head. Several small black spots along the sides of white tail.

Female: same as male, but lacks a red mark on head

Juvenile: same as female, some have a red mark near the forehead

Nest: cavity; male and female excavate; 1 brood per year

Eggs: 3-5; white without markings

Incubation: 11-12 days; female and male incubate, the female incubates during day, male at night

Fledging: 20-25 days; male and female feed young

Migration: non-migrator

Food: insects, seeds; visits seed and suet feeders

Compare: Almost identical to the Hairy Woodpecker (pg. 31), but smaller. Look for the shorter, thinner bill of Downy to differentiate them.

Stan's Notes: Abundant and widespread where trees are present. Stiff tail feathers help brace it like a tripod as it clings to a tree. Like all woodpeckers, it has a long barbed tongue to pull insects from tiny places. Male and female will drum on branches or hollow logs to announce territories, which are rarely larger than 5 acres (2 ha). Male performs most brooding. Will winter roost in cavity.

female
pg. 115

male

SUMMER

Rose-breasted Grosbeak
Pheucticus ludovicianus

Size: 7-8" (18-20 cm)

Male: A plump black-and-white bird with a large, triangular rose patch in the center of chest. Wing linings are rosy red. Large ivory bill.

Female: heavily streaked brown and white bird, large white eyebrows, orange yellow wing linings

Juvenile: similar to female

Nest: cup; female and male construct; 1-2 broods per year

Eggs: 3-5; blue green with brown markings

Incubation: 13-14 days; female and male incubate

Fledging: 9-12 days; female and male feed young

Migration: complete, to Mexico, Central America and South America

Food: insects, seeds, fruit; comes to seed feeders

Compare: Male is very distinctive with no look-alikes.

Stan's Notes: A summer resident, but more conspicuous when in small groups during migration. Usually prefers mature deciduous forest for nesting. Both sexes sing, but the male sings much louder and clearer. Has a rich, robin-like song. Common name "Grosbeak" refers to its large bill, used to crush seeds. Rose breast patch varies in size and shape in each male. Male has white wing patches, which flash in flight. Late to arrive in spring and early to leave in autumn. Males arrive in small groups first, joined by females several days later. Several males can be seen visiting seed feeders at the same time in spring. When the females arrive, males become territorial and reduce their visits to feeders. Young grosbeaks visit feeders with adults after fledging.

male

female

Yellow-bellied Sapsucker
Sphyrapicus varius

MIGRATION
SUMMER

Size: 8-9" (20-22.5 cm)

Male: Medium-sized woodpecker with checkered back. Has a red forehead, crown and chin. Tan-to-yellow breast and belly. White wing patches flash while flying.

Female: similar to male, white chin

Juvenile: similar to female, dull brown and lacks any red marking

Nest: cavity; female and male excavate; 1 brood per year

Eggs: 5-6; white without markings

Incubation: 12-13 days; female and male incubate, the female incubates during day, male at night

Fledging: 25-29 days; female and male feed young

Migration: complete, to southern states, Mexico and Central America

Food: insects, tree sap; comes to suet feeders

Compare: The male Yellow-bellied Sapsucker shares the red chin of Red-headed Woodpecker (pg. 33), but lacks an all-red head. Female Yellow-bellied Sapsucker has a white chin.

Stan's Notes: Drills holes in a pattern of horizontal rows in small-to medium-sized trees to bleed tree sap. Many birds drink from sapsucker taps. Oozing sap also attracts insects, which sapsuckers eat. Sapsuckers will defend their sapping sites from the other birds. They don't suck sap; rather, they lap it with their long tongues. A quiet bird with few vocalizations, but will mew like a cat. Unlike other woodpeckers, drumming rhythm is irregular.

male

female

YEAR-ROUND

Hairy Woodpecker
Picoides villosus

Size: 9" (22.5 cm)

Male: Black-and-white woodpecker with a white belly, and black wings with rows of white spots. White stripe down back. Long black bill. Red mark on back of head.

Female: same as male, but lacks a red mark on head

Juvenile: grayer version of female

Nest: cavity; female and male excavate; 1 brood per year

Eggs: 3-6; white without markings

Incubation: 11-15 days; female and male incubate, the female incubates during day, male at night

Fledging: 28-30 days; male and female feed young

Migration: non-migrator

Food: insects, nuts, seeds; comes to seed and suet feeders

Compare: Larger than Downy Woodpecker (pg. 25) and has a longer bill that is nearly the width of the head.

Stan's Notes: A common woodpecker of wooded backyards that announces its arrival with a sharp chirp before landing on feeders. This bird is responsible for eating many destructive forest insects. Has a barbed tongue, which helps it extract insects from trees. Tiny bristle-like feathers at the base of bill protect the nostrils from wood dust. Drums on hollow logs, branches or stovepipes in springtime to announce its territory. Often prefers to excavate nest cavities in live aspen trees. Has a larger, more oval-shaped cavity entrance than that of Downy Woodpecker.

juvenile

Red-headed Woodpecker
Melanerpes erythrocephalus

YEAR-ROUND

Size: 9" (22.5 cm)

Male: All-red head and a solid black back. White rump, chest and belly. Large white patches on wings flash when in flight. A black tail. Gray legs and bill.

Female: same as male

Juvenile: gray brown with white chest, lacks any red

Nest: cavity; male builds with help from female; 1 brood per year

Eggs: 4-5; white without markings

Incubation: 12-13 days; female and male incubate

Fledging: 27-30 days; female and male feed young

Migration: partial migrator; will move to areas with an abundant supply of nuts

Food: insects, nuts, fruit; comes to seed and suet feeders

Compare: No other woodpecker in New York has an all-red head. Pileated Woodpecker (pg. 45) is the only other woodpecker with a solid black back, but it has a partial red head.

Stan's Notes: One of the few woodpecker species in which male and female appear the same (look alike). Bill is not as well adapted for excavating holes as in other woodpeckers, so it chooses dead or rotten tree branches for nest. Later nesting than the closely related Red-bellied Woodpecker and will often take over its nesting cavity. Prefers more open or edge woodlands with many dead trees. Often seen perching on tops of dead snags. Stores acorns and other nuts. Decreasing populations nationwide.

CD 1, TRACK 16

33

male

female

Red-bellied Woodpecker
Melanerpes carolinus

YEAR-ROUND

Size: 9¼" (23 cm)

Male: "Zebra-backed" woodpecker with a white rump. Red crown extends down the nape of neck. Tan breast with a tinge of red on belly, which is often hard to see.

Female: same as male, but with a gray crown

Juvenile: gray version of adults, no red cap or nape

Nest: cavity; female and male excavate; 1 brood per year

Eggs: 4-5; white without markings

Incubation: 12-14 days; female and male incubate, the female incubates during day, male at night

Fledging: 24-27 days; female and male feed young

Migration: non-migrator; moves around to find food

Food: insects, nuts, fruit; comes to seed and suet feeders

Compare: Similar to Northern Flicker (pg. 137) and Yellow-bellied Sapsucker (pg. 29). Note the tan chest and belly with obvious black-and-white stripes on the back. The Red-headed Woodpecker (pg. 33) has an all-red head.

Stan's Notes: Named for its easily overlooked rosy red belly patch. Mostly a bird of shady woodlands. Excavates holes in rotten wood, looking for spiders, centipedes and beetles. Will hammer acorns and berries into crevices of trees for winter food. Returns to the same tree to excavate a new nest below that of the previous year. Often kicked out of nest hole by European Starlings. Gives a loud "querrr" call and a low "chug-chug-chug."

winter pg. 213

breeding

Black-bellied Plover
Pluvialis squatarola

MIGRATION
SUMMER

Size: 11-12" (28-30 cm)

Male: Striking black and white breeding plumage. A black belly, breast, sides, face and neck. White cap, nape of neck and belly near tail. Black legs and bill.

Female: less black on belly and breast than male

Juvenile: grayer than adults, with much less black

Nest: ground; male and female construct; 1 brood per year

Eggs: 3-4; pinkish or greenish with black brown markings

Incubation: 26-27 days; male and female incubate, male incubates during the day, female at night

Fledging: 35-45 days; male feeds young, young learn quickly to feed themselves

Migration: complete, to the East and Gulf coasts, West Indies, Mexico, Central and South America

Food: insects

Compare: The breeding Dunlin (pg. 121) is slightly smaller, with a rusty back and long down-curved bill. Look for a large black patch on the belly, face and chest and a white cap.

Stan's Notes: Male performs a "butterfly" courtship flight to attract females. Female leaves the male and young about 12 days after the eggs hatch. Starts breeding at 3 years of age. Begins fall migration in July and August. During flight, in any plumage, displays a white rump and stripe on wings with black axillaries (armpits). Will often dart across the ground to grab an insect and run.

female pg. 147

male

Lesser Scaup
Aythya affinis

WINTER

Size: 16-17" (40-43 cm)

Male: Appears mostly black with bold white sides and gray back. Chest and head look nearly black, but head appears purple with green highlights in direct sun. Bright yellow eyes.

Female: overall brown with dull white patch at base of light gray bill, yellow eyes

Juvenile: same as female

Nest: ground; female builds; 1 brood per year

Eggs: 8-14; olive buff without markings

Incubation: 22-28 days; female incubates

Fledging: 45-50 days; female teaches young to feed

Migration: complete, to New York and southern states

Food: aquatic plants and insects

Compare: Similar to the male Common Goldeneye (pg. 47), which is larger. Male Blue-winged Teal (pg. 145) is slightly smaller and has a bright white crescent-shaped mark at base of bill. Look for bold white sides and a gray back to help identify the male Scaup.

Stan's Notes: A common diving duck. Often in large flocks along western Lake Erie each spring. Mostly seen when it migrates in late February and October. Submerges to feed on the bottom of lakes (unlike dabbling ducks, which tip forward to reach bottom). Note the bold white stripe under wings when in flight. Male leaves female when she starts to incubate her eggs. Quantity of eggs (clutch size) increases with age of female. Interesting baby-sitting arrangement in which groups of young (crèches) are tended by 1-3 adult females.

female pg. 153

male

Hooded Merganser
Lophodytes cucullatus

MIGRATION WINTER

Size: 16-19" (40-48 cm)

Male: A sleek black-and-white bird that has rusty brown sides. Crest "hood" raises to reveal a large white patch. Long, thin black bill.

Female: sleek brown and rust bird with a ragged rusty crest and long, thin brown bill

Juvenile: similar to female

Nest: cavity; female lines old woodpecker hole; 1 brood per year

Eggs: 10-12; white without markings

Incubation: 32-33 days; female incubates

Fledging: 71 days; female feeds young

Migration: complete, to Long Island, southern states

Food: small fish, aquatic insects

Compare: A distinctive diving bird. Smaller than male Common Merganser (pg. 237). Look for the male's large white patch on the head and rusty brown sides. The male Wood Duck (pg. 231) has a similar size and green head.

Stan's Notes: A small diving bird of shallow ponds, sloughs, lakes and rivers. Male Hooded Merganser can voluntarily raise and lower its crest to show off the large white head patch. Rarely found away from wooded areas, where it nests in natural cavities or nest boxes. Female will "dump" her eggs into other female Hooded Merganser nests, resulting in 20-25 eggs in some nests. Known to share nest cavities with Common Goldeneyes and Wood Ducks, sitting side by side. Not as common as the Common Merganser.

American Oystercatcher
Haematopus palliatus

SUMMER

Size: 18-19" (45-48 cm)

Male: Large shorebird with a large red-orange bill, black head and dark brown sides, wings and back. White chest and belly. Pink legs. Red ring around the eyes.

Female: same as male

Juvenile: more gray than black and lacks the brightly colored bill

Nest: ground; male and female construct; 1 brood per year

Eggs: 2-4; olive with sparse brown markings

Incubation: 24-29 days; male and female incubate, male incubates during the day, female at night

Fledging: 35-40 days; male and female feed young, young learn quickly to feed themselves

Migration: complete, to the East and Gulf coasts, West Indies, Mexico, Central and South America

Food: shellfish, insects, aquatic insects, worms

Compare: Larger than breeding Black-bellied Plover (pg. 37). Look for the large and obvious red-orange bill of Oystercatcher to identify.

Stan's Notes: This large, chunky shorebird has a flattened, heavy bill, which it uses to pry open shellfish and probe sand for insects and worms. Can be categorized according to its preferred oyster-opening technique. Stabbers sneak up on mollusks and stab their bills between shells before they have a chance to close. Hammerers shatter one-half of the shell with several direct, powerful blows.

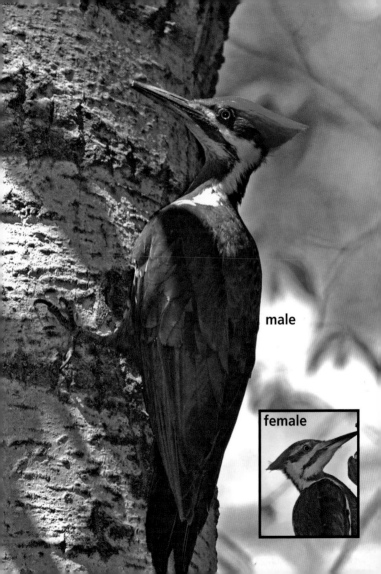

male

female

Pileated Woodpecker
Dryocopus pileatus

YEAR-ROUND

Size: 19" (48 cm)

Male: Crow-sized woodpecker with a black back and bright red crest. Long gray bill with red mustache. White leading edge of the wings flashes brightly when flying.

Female: same as male, but has a black forehead and lacks red mustache

Juvenile: similar to adults, only duller and browner

Nest: cavity; male and female excavate; 1 brood per year

Eggs: 3-5; white without markings

Incubation: 15-18 days; female and male incubate, the female incubates during day, male at night

Fledging: 26-28 days; female and male feed young

Migration: non-migrator

Food: insects; will come to suet feeders

Compare: Red-headed Woodpecker (pg. 33) is about half the size and has an all-red head, black back and white rump. Look for the bright red crest and exceptionally large size of the Pileated Woodpecker.

Stan's Notes: Our largest woodpecker. The common name comes from the Latin *pileatus*, which means "wearing a cap," referring to its crest. A relatively shy bird that prefers large tracts of woodland. Drums on hollow branches, chimneys, etc., to announce territory. Excavates oval holes up to several feet long in tree trunks, looking for insects to eat. Large chips of wood lie at bases of excavated trees. Favorite food is carpenter ants. Young are fed regurgitated insects.

male

female pg. 157

Common Goldeneye

Bucephala clangula

MIGRATION
SUMMER
WINTER

Size: 18½-20" (47-50 cm)

Male: A mostly white duck with a black back and large, puffy green head. Large white spot in front of each bright golden eye. Dark bill.

Female: brown and gray, a large dark brown head, gray body, white collar, bright golden eyes, yellow-tipped dark bill

Juvenile: same as female, but has a dark bill

Nest: cavity; female lines old woodpecker cavity; 1 brood per year

Eggs: 8-10; light green without markings

Incubation: 28-32 days; female incubates

Fledging: 56-59 days; female leads young to food

Migration: complete, to New York, southern states and Mexico

Food: aquatic plants, insects

Compare: Similar to the black and white male Lesser Scaup (pg. 39), which is smaller. Look for a white chest and a distinctive white mark in front of each golden eye.

Stan's Notes: Known for its loud whistling, produced by its wings in flight. In late winter and early spring, male often attracts female through elaborate displays, throwing its head backward while it utters a single raspy note. Female will lay eggs in other goldeneye nests, which results in some mothers incubating up to 30 eggs. Received the common name from its obvious bright golden eyes. Winters in parts of New York where it finds open water.

soaring

MIGRATION SUMMER

Osprey
Pandion haliaetus

Size: 24" (60 cm); up to 5½-foot wingspan

Male: Large eagle-like bird with a white chest and belly and a nearly black back. White head with a black streak through the eyes. Large wings with black "wrist" marks. Dark bill.

Female: same as male, but larger with a necklace of brown streaking

Juvenile: similar to adults, with a light tan breast

Nest: platform, often on raised wooden platform; female and male build; 1 brood per year

Eggs: 2-4; white with brown markings

Incubation: 32-42 days; female and male incubate

Fledging: 48-58 days; male and female feed young

Migration: complete, to southern states, Mexico and Central and South America

Food: fish

Compare: Bald Eagle (pg. 55) is on average 10 inches (25 cm) larger with an all-white head and tail. The juvenile Bald Eagle is brown with white speckles. Look for a white belly and dark stripe through eyes to identify Osprey.

Stan's Notes: Ospreys are in a family all their own. It is the only raptor that plunges into water feet first to catch fish. Can hover for a few seconds before diving. Carries fish in a head-first position for better aerodynamics. Often harassed by Bald Eagles for its catch. In flight, wings are angled (cocked) backward. Nests on man-made towers and in tall dead trees. Recent studies show male and female might mate for life. May not migrate to same wintering grounds.

winter

breeding

MIGRATION
SUMMER

Common Loon
Gavia immer

Size: 28-36" (71-90 cm)

Male: Breeding adult has a black-and-white back with a checkerboard pattern, a black head, white necklace, deep red eyes and a long, pointed black bill. Winter adult has an all-gray body and bill.

Female: same as male

Juvenile: similar to winter adult, lacks red eyes

Nest: platform, on the ground; female and male build; 1 brood per year

Eggs: 2; olive brown, occasionally brown markings

Incubation: 26-31 days; female and male incubate

Fledging: 75-80 days; female and male feed young

Migration: complete, to southern states, the Gulf coast and Mexico

Food: fish, aquatic insects

Compare: Double-crested Cormorant (pg. 21) has a black chest and gray bill with yellow at the base and a hooked tip.

Stan's Notes: A true symbol of the wildness of our lakes. Prefers clear lakes because it hunts for fish by eyesight. Legs are set so far back that it has a difficult time walking on land, but it is a great swimmer. Common name comes from the Swedish word *lom*, meaning "lame," for the awkward way it walks on land. Its unique call suggests the wild laughter of a demented person and led to the phrase "crazy as a loon." Young ride on backs of swimming parents. Adults perform distraction displays to protect young. Very sensitive to disturbance during nesting and will abandon nest.

 CD 1, TRACK 25

juvenile

breeding

Great Black-backed Gull
Larus marinus

YEAR-ROUND

Size: 30" (76 cm); up to 5½-foot wingspan

Male: A very large gull. Black and white breeding plumage with a white head, chest and belly and black back and wings. Has a distinctive yellow bill with an orange mark close to the end of the lower bill. Pink legs.

Female: same as male

Juvenile: gray and brown, lacks any large black spots, has a gray bill

Nest: ground; male and female construct; 1 brood per year

Eggs: 2-3; olive with sparse brown markings

Incubation: 26-29 days; female and male incubate

Fledging: 49-56 days; male and female feed young

Migration: non-migrator in New York

Food: fish, insects, crustaceans

Compare: Larger than the Ring-billed Gull (pg. 263), Herring Gull (pg. 265) and Laughing Gull (pg. 261). Look for a white head, black back and bright yellow bill with an orange spot.

Stan's Notes: One of the largest gulls. A four-year gull, meaning it undergoes four distinct color phases to reach adulthood. Phases are often hard to distinguish and depend upon the amount of black on the bird. First-year gull lacks black on the back and has a gray bill. Second summer gull has small amounts of black and a pale yellow bill with a black tip. Third summer gull has much more black on the back and wings and a black-tipped yellow bill. Fourth summer gull or breeding adult has a black back and wings.

CD 1, TRACK 26

soaring

juvenile

soaring
juvenile

Bald Eagle
Haliaeetus leucocephalus

YEAR-ROUND
MIGRATION

Size: 31-37" (79-94 cm); up to 7-foot wingspan

Male: Pure white head and tail contrast with dark brown-to-black body and wings. A large, curved yellow bill and yellow feet.

Female: same as male, only slightly larger

Juvenile: dark brown with white spots or speckles throughout body and wings, gray bill

Nest: massive platform, usually in a tree; female and male build; 1 brood per year

Eggs: 2; off-white without markings

Incubation: 34-36 days; female and male incubate

Fledging: 75-90 days; female and male feed young

Migration: non-migrator to partial in New York

Food: fish, carrion, birds (mainly ducks)

Compare: Turkey Vulture (pg. 19) lacks the adult Bald Eagle's white head and tail. Turkey Vulture is smaller, has two-toned wings and flies with its wings held in a V shape unlike the straight-out wing position of the Bald Eagle.

Stan's Notes: Driven to near extinction due to DDT poisoning and illegal killing. Now making a comeback in North America. Returns to same nest each year, adding more sticks, enlarging it to massive proportions, at times up to 1,000 pounds (450 kg). In the midair mating ritual, one eagle will flip upside down and lock talons with another. Both tumble, then break apart to continue flight. Thought to mate for life, but will switch mates if not successful reproducing. Juvenile attains the white head and tail at about 4-5 years of age.

CD 1, TRACK 27

SUMMER

Tree Swallow
Tachycineta bicolor

Size: 5-6" (13-15 cm)

Male: Blue green during spring and greener in fall. Appears to change color in direct sunlight. White chin, breast and belly. Long, pointed wing tips. Notched tail.

Female: similar to male, only duller

Juvenile: gray brown with a white belly and grayish breast band

Nest: cavity; female and male line former woodpecker cavity or nest box; 1 brood per year

Eggs: 4-6; white without markings

Incubation: 13-16 days; female incubates

Fledging: 20-24 days; female and male feed young

Migration: complete, to Mexico and Central America

Food: insects

Compare: Similar color as Purple Martin (pg. 65), but smaller with a white breast and belly. The Barn Swallow (pg. 61) has a rust belly and deeply forked tail.

Stan's Notes: The first swallow species to return each spring. Most common at agricultural fields, ponds, lakes and coastal beaches. Will compete with bluebirds for cavities and nest boxes. Can be attracted to your yard with a nest box. Travels great distances to find dropped feathers to line its grass nest. Sometimes seen playing, chasing after dropped feathers. Often seen flying back and forth across fields, feeding on insects. Gathers in large flocks to migrate.

male

female pg. 93

Indigo Bunting
Passerina cyanea

SUMMER

Size: 5½" (14 cm)

Male: Vibrant blue finch-like bird. Scattered dark markings on wings and tail.

Female: light brown bird with faint markings

Juvenile: similar to female

Nest: cup; female builds; 2 broods per year

Eggs: 3-4; pale blue without markings

Incubation: 12-13 days; female incubates

Fledging: 10-11 days; female feeds young

Migration: complete, to southern Florida, Mexico and Central and South America

Food: insects, seeds, fruit; will visit seed feeders

Compare: Male Eastern Bluebird (pg. 63) is larger and has a rusty red breast.

Stan's Notes: Usually only the males are noticed. Actually a black bird, as it doesn't have any blue pigment in its feathers. As with the Blue Jay, sunlight is refracted within the structure of the bunting's feathers, making them appear blue. Appears iridescent in direct sun. Molts to acquire body feathers with gray tips, which quickly wear off to reveal bright blue plumage in spring. Molts in fall to appear like females during winter. Males often sing from treetops to attract mates. Will come to feeders in spring before insects are plentiful. Mostly seen along woodland edges, feeding on insects. Migrates at night in flocks of 5-10 individuals. A late migrant, males return before females and juveniles, usually returning to previous year's nest site. Juveniles move to within a mile from birth site.

CD 1, TRACK 29

SUMMER

Barn Swallow
Hirundo rustica

Size: 7" (18 cm)

Male: A sleek swallow. Blue black back, cinnamon belly and reddish brown chin. White spots on a long, deeply forked tail.

Female: same as male, only slightly duller

Juvenile: similar to adults, with a tan belly and chin and a shorter tail

Nest: cup; female and male construct; 2 broods per year

Eggs: 4-5; white with brown markings

Incubation: 13-17 days; female incubates

Fledging: 18-23 days; female and male feed young

Migration: complete, to South America

Food: insects, prefers beetles, wasps and flies

Compare: The Tree Swallow (pg. 57) has a white belly and chin and a notched tail. The Chimney Swift (pg. 75) has a narrow pointed tail and longer wings than its body. Purple Martin (pg. 65) is larger, with a dark purple belly.

Stan's Notes: Of the six swallow species in New York, this is the only one with a deeply forked tail. Unlike other swallows, the Barn Swallow rarely glides in flight, so look for continuous flapping. It builds a mud nest using up to 1,000 beak-loads of mud, often in or on barns. Nests in colonies of 4-6 individuals, but nesting alone isn't uncommon. Drinks in flight, skimming water or getting water from wet leaves. Also bathes while flying through rain or sprinklers.

YEAR-ROUND
SUMMER

Eastern Bluebird
Sialia sialis

Size: 7" (18 cm)

Male: Reminiscent of its larger cousin, American Robin, with a rusty red breast and a white belly. Sky blue head, back and tail.

Female: shares rusty red breast and white belly, but is grayer with faint blue tail and wings

Juvenile: similar to female, with spots on chest, blue wing markings

Nest: cavity, old woodpecker cavity or man-made nest box; female builds; 2 broods per year

Eggs: 4-5; pale blue without markings

Incubation: 12-14 days; female incubates

Fledging: 15-18 days; male and female feed young

Migration: partial to non-migrator in New York

Food: insects, fruit

Compare: Male Indigo Bunting (pg. 59) is nearly all blue, lacking the rusty red breast. Blue Jay (pg. 67) is much larger and has a crest.

Stan's Notes: Once nearly eliminated from New York due to a lack of nest cavities, bluebirds have made a remarkable comeback with the aid of bird enthusiasts who have put up thousands of bluebird nest boxes. Easily tamed, it will come to a shallow dish with mealworms. Bluebirds like open habitats such as farm fields, pastures and roadsides. Will perch in trees or on fence posts and wait for grasshoppers. Sings a distinctive "chur-lee chur chur-lee." Gathers in large family groups to migrate. Males return first in springtime, followed by females a week or two later. Young of the first brood help raise young of the second.

CD 1, TRACK 31

male

female

Purple Martin
Progne subis

Size: 8½" (22 cm)

Male: A large swallow-shaped bird with a purple head, back and belly. Black wings and tail. Notched tail.

Female: gray purple head and back with a whitish belly, darker wings and tail

Juvenile: same as female

Nest: cavity; female and male line cavity of house; 1 brood per year

Eggs: 4-5; white without markings

Incubation: 15-18 days; female incubates

Fledging: 26-30 days; male and female feed young

Migration: complete, to South America

Food: insects

Compare: The male is the only swallow with a dark purple belly. Usually seen only in groups.

Stan's Notes: The largest swallow species in North America. Once nested in tree cavities, but now nearly exclusively nests in man-made nest boxes in New York. Main diet consists of dragonflies, not mosquitoes as once thought. Often drinks and bathes while flying by skimming water or flying through rain. Returns to the same nest site each year. Males arrive before the females and yearlings. Often nests within 100 feet (30 m) of a human dwelling and, in fact, the most successful colonies are located within this distance. Young strike out to form new colonies. Huge colonies gather in the fall to migrate to South America.

CD 1, TRACK 32

YEAR-ROUND

Blue Jay
Cyanocitta cristata

Size: 12" (30 cm)

Male: Large, bright light blue and white bird with a black necklace. Crest moves up and down at will. White face with a gray belly. White wing bars on blue wings. Black spots and a white tip on blue tail.

Female: same as male

Juvenile: same as adult, only duller

Nest: cup; female and male construct; 1-2 broods per year

Eggs: 4-5; green to blue with brown markings

Incubation: 16-18 days; female incubates

Fledging: 17-21 days; female and male feed young

Migration: non-migrator to partial; will move around to find an abundant food source

Food: insects, fruit, carrion, seeds, nuts; comes to seed feeders, and ground feeders with corn

Compare: Eastern Bluebird (pg. 63) is much smaller and lacks the Jay's white markings and crest. Belted Kingfisher (pg. 69) lacks the vivid blue coloring and black necklace of the Jay.

Stan's Notes: Highly intelligent bird, solving problems, gathering food and communicating more than other birds. Will scream like a hawk to scatter birds at a feeder. Known as the alarm of the forest, screaming at intruders in woods. Known to eat eggs or young birds from the nests of other birds. One of the few birds to cache food. Feathers don't have blue pigment; refracted sunlight casts blue light.

male

female

SUMMER

Belted Kingfisher

Ceryle alcyon

Size: 13" (33 cm)

Male: Large blue bird with white belly. Broad blue gray breast band and a ragged crest that is raised and lowered at will. Large head with a long, thick black bill. A small white spot directly in front of red brown eyes. Black wing tips with splashes of white that flash when flying.

Female: same as male, but with rusty breast band in addition to blue gray band, and rusty flanks

Juvenile: similar to female

Nest: cavity; female and male excavate; 1 brood per year

Eggs: 6-7; white without markings

Incubation: 23-24 days; female and male incubate

Fledging: 23-24 days; female and male feed young

Migration: complete, to southern states, Mexico and Central and South America

Food: small fish

Compare: Kingfisher is darker blue than the Blue Jay (pg. 67) and has a larger, more ragged crest. Kingfisher is rarely found away from water.

Stan's Notes: Seen perched on branches close to water, it will dive headfirst for small fish and return to a branch to eat. Has a loud machine-gun-like call. Excavates a deep cavity in bank of river or lake. Parents drop dead fish into water, teaching the young to dive. Regurgitates pellets of bone after meals, being unable to pass bones through the digestive tract. Mates recognize each other by call.

Chestnut-sided Warbler
Dendroica pensylvanica

SUMMER

Size: 5" (13 cm)

Male: A colorful combination of a yellow cap and black mask set against a white face, chin, breast and belly. Two yellow wing bars on gray wings. Chestnut flanks.

Female: similar to male, flanks are duller brown

Juvenile: similar to female, has a lime green head and back, a white eye-ring, bright yellow wing bars, lacks chestnut sides

Nest: cup; female builds; 1 brood per year

Eggs: 3-5; white with brown markings

Incubation: 12-13 days; female incubates

Fledging: 10-12 days; female and male feed young

Migration: complete, to Central America

Food: insects, berries

Compare: Shares the yellow cap with Yellow-rumped Warbler (pg. 185), but lacks yellow sides and rump. The Yellow Warbler (pg. 279) is nearly all yellow and lacks Chestnut-sided's white chest and chestnut flanks.

Stan's Notes: Prefers an open, young aspen forest. Often attracted to backyard water gardens during migration. Look for this attractive warbler in spring, hopping high in the branches while it hunts for insects. You'll usually only get a glimpse of this fast-moving warbler. Will hold tail in an uplifted position, showing its white undertail. Not uncommon for it to approach humans in defense of a nest site.

Brown Creeper
Certhia americana

Size: 5" (13 cm)

Male: Small, thin, nearly camouflaged brown bird. White from chin to belly. White eyebrows. Long stiff tail. Dark eyes. Thin curved bill.

Female: same as male

Juvenile: same as adult

Nest: cup; female builds; unknown how many broods per year

Eggs: 5-6; white with tiny brown markings

Incubation: 14-17 days; female incubates, male feeds female during incubation

Fledging: 13-16 days; female and male feed young

Migration: non-migrator to partial in New York

Food: insects, nuts, seeds

Compare: Creeps up tree trunks, not down, like the White-breasted Nuthatch (pg. 189). Watch for the Brown Creeper to fly from the top of one trunk to the bottom of another, then work its way to the top, looking for insects. Slightly larger than Red-breasted Nuthatch (pg. 181), with a similar white stripe above the eyes, but the Brown Creeper has a white belly, long tail and lacks a black crown.

Stan's Notes: This bird utilizes its camouflage coloring to defend itself, spreading out flat on a branch or tree trunk without moving. Young are able to follow their parents, creeping soon after fledging. Commonly found in wooded areas. Often builds nest behind loose bark of dead or dying trees.

CD 1, TRACK 36

SUMMER

Chimney Swift
Chaetura pelagica

Size: 5" (13 cm)

Male: Nondescript, swallow-shaped bird, usually seen only in flight. Long, thin brown body with a pointed tail and head. Long swept-back wings, longer than the body.

Female: same as male

Juvenile: same as adult

Nest: half cup; female and male build; 1 brood per year

Eggs: 4-5; white without markings

Incubation: 19-21 days; female and male incubate

Fledging: 28-30 days; female and male feed young

Migration: complete, to South America

Food: insects caught in air

Compare: Considerably smaller than Purple Martin (pg. 65) and lacks the iridescent purple of the Martin. The Barn Swallow (pg. 61) has a forked tail unlike the pointed tail of the Chimney Swift. Tree Swallow (pg. 57) has a white belly and blue green back.

Stan's Notes: One of the fastest fliers in the bird world. Spends all day flying, rarely perching. Bathes and drinks by skimming across water surfaces. Unique in-flight twittering call is often heard before bird is seen. Flies in groups, feeding on flying insects nearly 100 feet (30 m) in the air. Often called Flying Cigar due to its pointed body shape. Hundreds will nest and roost in large chimneys, hence the common name. Builds nest with tiny twigs, cementing it with saliva, attaching it to the inside of a chimney or hollow tree.

SUMMER

Chipping Sparrow
Spizella passerina

Size: 5" (13 cm)

Male: Small gray brown sparrow with a clear gray breast, rusty crown and white eyebrows. A black eye line and thin gray black bill. Two faint wing bars.

Female: same as male

Juvenile: similar to adult, has a streaked breast, lacks the rusty crown

Nest: cup; female builds; 2 broods per year

Eggs: 3-5; blue green with brown markings

Incubation: 11-14 days; female incubates

Fledging: 10-12 days; female and male feed young

Migration: complete, to southern states, Mexico and Central America

Food: insects, seeds; will come to ground feeders

Compare: The American Tree Sparrow (pg. 97) shares a rusty crown, but lacks the black eye line. Fox Sparrow (pg. 105) lacks a clear breast. The Song Sparrow (pg. 89) has a heavily streaked breast. The female House Finch (pg. 81) also has a streaked breast.

Stan's Notes: A common garden or yard bird, often seen feeding on dropped seeds beneath feeders. Gathers in large family groups to feed in preparation for migration. Migrates at night in flocks of 20-30 birds. The common name comes from the male's fast "chip" call. Often is just called Chippy. Nest is placed low in dense shrubs and is almost always lined with animal hair. Can be very unafraid of people, allowing you to approach closely before it flies away.

male

female

Common Redpoll
Carduelis flammea

Size: 5" (13 cm)

Male: A small sparrow-like bird with a bright red crown and black spot on the chin. Heavily streaked back and a splash of raspberry red on the chest.

Female: same as male, but lacking raspberry red on the chest

Juvenile: browner than adults, lacks a red crown, has dark streaks on the chest

Nest: cup; female builds; 1 brood (sometimes 2) per year

Eggs: 4-5; pale green with purple markings

Incubation: 10-11 days; female incubates

Fledging: 11-12 days; female and male feed young

Migration: irruptive; moves from Canada into New York in some winters

Food: seeds, insects; will come to seed feeders

Compare: Slightly smaller than the male Purple Finch (pg. 249), lacking male Purple Finch's red back and rump. Similar to the male House Finch (pg. 247), but lacks the orange red rump. Look for the bright red crown and black spot under the bill.

Stan's Notes: Name is derived from the color and "taking a poll" or counting heads. This bird winters in the state after summering in the far reaches of Canada. Winter flocks of up to 100 birds are not uncommon. Bathes in snow or open water in winter. Much like the Black-capped Chickadee, it can be tamed and hand fed.

male
pg. 247

female

House Finch
Carpodacus mexicanus

YEAR-ROUND

Size: 5" (13 cm)

Female: A plain brown bird with a heavily streaked white chest.

Male: orange red face, chest and rump, a brown cap, brown marking behind eyes, brown wings streaked with white, streaked belly

Juvenile: similar to female

Nest: cup, occasionally in a cavity; female builds; 2 broods per year

Eggs: 4-5; pale blue, lightly marked

Incubation: 12-14 days; female incubates

Fledging: 15-19 days; female and male feed young

Migration: non-migrator to partial; will move around to find food

Food: seeds, fruit, leaf buds; will visit seed feeders

Compare: The female Purple Finch (pg. 95) is very similar, but has bold white eyebrows. The female American Goldfinch (pg. 273) has a clear chest and white wing bars. Similar to Pine Siskin (pg. 85), but lacks yellow wing bars and has a much larger bill than Siskin.

Stan's Notes: Very social bird. Visits feeders in small flocks. Likes nesting in hanging flower baskets. Incubating female is fed by the male. Has a loud, cheerful warbling song. House Finches that were originally introduced to Long Island, New York, from the western U.S. in the 1940s have since populated the entire eastern U.S. Now found across the country. Can be the most common bird at feeders. Suffers from a fatal eye disease that causes the eyes to crust over.

SUMMER

House Wren
Troglodytes aedon

Size: 5" (13 cm)

Male: A small all-brown bird with lighter brown markings on tail and wings. Slightly curved brown bill. Often holds its tail erect.

Female: same as male

Juvenile: same as adult

Nest: cavity; female and male line just about any nest cavity; 2 broods per year

Eggs: 4-6; tan with brown markings

Incubation: 10-13 days; female and male incubate

Fledging: 12-15 days; female and male feed young

Migration: complete, to southern states and Mexico

Food: insects, spiders, snails

Compare: House Wren is distinguished from Carolina Wren (pg. 87) by the lack of eyebrows. The long curved bill and long upturned tail of House Wren differentiates it from sparrows.

Stan's Notes: A prolific songster, it will sing from dawn until dusk during the mating season. Easily attracted to nest boxes. In spring, the male chooses several prospective nesting cavities and places a few small twigs in each. Female inspects each, chooses one, and finishes the nest building. She will completely fill the nest cavity with uniformly small twigs, then line a small depression at back of cavity with pine needles and grass. Often has trouble fitting long twigs through nest cavity hole. Tries many different directions and approaches until successful.

YEAR-ROUND
WINTER

Pine Siskin
Carduelis pinus

Size: 5" (13 cm)

Male: Small brown finch. Heavily streaked back, breast and belly. Yellow wing bars. Yellow at base of tail. Thin bill.

Female: similar to male, with less yellow

Juvenile: similar to adult, light yellow tinge over the breast and chin

Nest: modified cup; female constructs; 2 broods per year

Eggs: 3-4; greenish blue with brown markings

Incubation: 12-13 days; female incubates

Fledging: 14-15 days; female and male feed young

Migration: irruptive; moves around the state in search of food

Food: seeds, insects; will come to seed feeders

Compare: Female American Goldfinch (pg. 273) lacks streaks and has white wing bars. Female House Finch (pg. 81) has a streaked chest, but lacks yellow wing bars. Female Purple Finch (pg. 95) has bold white eyebrows.

Stan's Notes: Usually considered a winter finch, seen in flocks of up to 20 individuals, often with other finch species. More commonly seen in northern half of New York, but can be found throughout the state during heavy invasion years. Comes to thistle feeders. Travels and breeds in small groups. Male feeds female during incubation. Juveniles lose the yellow tint by late summer of the first year. Builds nest toward ends of coniferous branches, where needles are dense, helping to conceal. Nests are often only a few feet apart.

Carolina Wren
Thryothorus ludovicianus

YEAR-ROUND

Size: 5½" (14 cm)

Male: Warm rusty brown head and back with an orange yellow chest and belly. White throat and a prominent white eye stripe. A short stubby tail, often cocked up.

Female: same as male

Juvenile: same as adult

Nest: cavity; female and male build; 2 broods per year, sometimes 3

Eggs: 4-6; white, sometimes pink or creamy, with brown markings

Incubation: 12-14 days; female incubates

Fledging: 12-14 days; female and male feed young

Migration: non-migrator

Food: insects, fruit, few seeds; visits suet feeders

Compare: Similar to House Wren (pg. 83), but the Carolina Wren is lighter brown and has a prominent white eye stripe.

Stan's Notes: Mates are long-term, remaining together throughout the year in permanent territories. Sings year-round. Male is known to sing up to 40 different song types, singing one song repeatedly before switching to another. Female also sings, resulting in duets. The male often takes over feeding the first brood while the female renests. Nests in birdhouses, unusual places such as in mailboxes, bumpers of cars or broken taillights, or in nearly any other cavity. Found in brushy yards or woodlands. Range expands northward in years with mild winters.

YEAR-ROUND
SUMMER

Song Sparrow
Melospiza melodia

Size: 5½" (14 cm)

Male: Common brown sparrow with heavy dark streaks on breast coalescing into a central dark spot.

Female: same as male

Juvenile: similar to adult, finely streaked breast, lacks a central spot

Nest: cup; female builds; 2 broods per year

Eggs: 3-4; pale blue to green with reddish brown markings

Incubation: 12-14 days; female incubates

Fledging: 9-12 days; female and male feed young

Migration: non-migrator to partial in New York

Food: insects, seeds; rarely visits seed feeders

Compare: Similar to other brown sparrows. Look for a heavily streaked chest with central dark spot.

Stan's Notes: Many subspecies or varieties of Song Sparrow, but the dark central spot is found in each variant. Returns to a similar area each year, defending a small territory by singing from thick shrubs. This is a constant songster that repeats its loud, clear song every couple minutes. Song varies in structure, but is basically the same from region to region. A ground feeder, look for it to scratch at the same time with both feet ("double-scratch") to expose seeds. While the female builds another nest for a second brood, the male often takes over feeding the young. Unlike many other sparrow species, Song Sparrows rarely flock together. A common host of the Brown-headed Cowbird.

male pg. 187

female

Dark-eyed Junco

Junco hyemalis

YEAR-ROUND WINTER

Size: 5½" (14 cm)

Female: Round, dark-eyed bird with a tan-to-brown chest, head and back. White belly. Ivory-to-pink bill. Since the outermost tail feathers are white, tail appears as a white V in flight.

Male: same as female, only slate gray to charcoal

Juvenile: similar to female, but has a streaked breast and head

Nest: cup; female and male construct; 2 broods per year

Eggs: 3-5; white with reddish brown markings

Incubation: 12-13 days; female incubates

Fledging: 10-13 days; male and female feed young

Migration: complete, across the U.S., non-migrator in parts of New York

Food: seeds, insects; will come to seed feeders

Compare: Rarely confused with any other bird. Small flocks feed under bird feeders in winter.

Stan's Notes: One of the most common winter birds in New York. Migrates from Canada to New York and beyond. Small population stays in the state year-round. Females tend to migrate farther south than the males. Adheres to a rigid social hierarchy, with dominant birds chasing the less dominant birds. Look for its white outer tail feathers flashing when in flight. Usually seen in small flocks on the ground, where it "double-scratches" with both feet simultaneously to expose seeds and insects. Eats many weed seeds. Nests in a wide variety of wooded habitats. Several junco species have now been combined into one, simply called Dark-eyed Junco.

CD 1, TRACK 45

female

male
pg. 59

Indigo Bunting
Passerina cyanea

SUMMER

Size: 5½" (14 cm)

Female: Light brown finch-like bird. Faint streaking on a light tan chest. Wings have a very faint blue cast with indistinct wing bars.

Male: vibrant blue finch-like bird, scattered dark markings on wings and tail

Juvenile: similar to female

Nest: cup; female builds; 2 broods per year

Eggs: 3-4; pale blue without markings

Incubation: 12-13 days; female incubates

Fledging: 10-11 days; female feeds young

Migration: complete, to southern Florida, Mexico and Central and South America

Food: insects, seeds, fruit; will visit seed feeders

Compare: Similar to female finches. Female American Goldfinch (pg. 273) has white wing bars. The female Purple Finch (pg. 95) has white eyebrows and a heavily streaked breast. The female House Finch (pg. 81) also has a heavily streaked breast.

Stan's Notes: A secretive bird, usually only the male buntings are seen. Males often sing from treetops to attract mates. Will come to feeders in the spring before insects are plentiful. Mostly seen along woodland edges, feeding on insects. Migrates at night in flocks of 5-10 individuals. A late migrant, males return before females and juveniles, usually returning to the previous year's nest site. Juveniles move to within a mile from birth site.

male pg. 249

female

Purple Finch
Carpodacus purpureus

YEAR-ROUND WINTER

Size: 6" (15 cm)

Female: A plain brown bird with a heavily streaked chest. Prominent white eyebrows.

Male: raspberry red head, cap, breast, back and rump, brownish wings and tail

Juvenile: same as female

Nest: cup; female and male construct; 1 brood per year

Eggs: 4-5; greenish blue with brown markings

Incubation: 12-13 days; female incubates

Fledging: 13-14 days; female and male feed young

Migration: irruptive; moves around in search of food

Food: seeds, insects, fruit; comes to seed feeders

Compare: Female House Finch (pg. 81) lacks female Purple Finch's white eyebrows. Pine Siskin (pg. 85) has yellow wing bars and a much smaller bill than the Purple Finch. Female American Goldfinch (pg. 273) has a clear chest and white wing bars.

Stan's Notes: A year-round resident in over half of New York. More commonly seen during migration in the rest of the state. In some parts of New York, often seen only in winter when flocks of Purple Finches leave their northern homes and move around searching for food. Visits seed feeders with House Finches, making it difficult to tell them apart. Eats mainly seeds. Prefers open woods or woodland edges. Travels in flocks of up to 50 birds. Has a rich loud song, with a distinctive "tic" note made only in flight. Not a purple color, Latin species name *purpureus* means "crimson" or other reddish color.

side view

front view

American Tree Sparrow
Spizella arborea

WINTER

Size: 6" (15 cm)

Male: Common brown sparrow with a tan breast and rusty crown. Black spot in the center of breast. Upper bill is dark, lower bill yellow. Two white wing bars. Gray eyebrows.

Female: same as male

Juvenile: lacks a rust crown, has a streaked chest that often obscures the central dark spot

Nest: cup; female builds; 1 brood per year

Eggs: 3-5; green white with brown markings

Incubation: 12-13 days; female incubates

Fledging: 8-10 days; female and male feed young

Migration: complete, throughout North America

Food: insects, seeds; visits seed feeders

Compare: Appears similar to other sparrows, so look closely at the center of breast for a single dark spot. Shares the rusty crown with the Chipping Sparrow (pg. 77), but lacks the Chippy's distinctive white eyebrows and black eye line. Song Sparrow (pg. 89) has a heavily streaked chest.

Stan's Notes: Seen mostly during migration in flocks ranging from 2-200. A bird feeder visitor throughout New York during winter. Occasionally called Winter Chippy because it looks similar to the Chipping Sparrow, a summer visitor. Nests in northern Canada and Alaska.

male

female

House Sparrow
Passer domesticus

YEAR-ROUND

Size: 6" (15 cm)

Male: Medium sparrow-like bird with large black spot on throat extending down to the chest. Brown back and single white wing bars. A gray belly and crown.

Female: slightly smaller than the male, light brown, lacks the throat patch and single wing bars

Juvenile: similar to female

Nest: domed cup nest, within cavity; female and male build; 2-3 broods per year

Eggs: 4-6; white with brown markings

Incubation: 10-12 days; female incubates

Fledging: 14-17 days; female and male feed young

Migration: non-migrator; moves around to find food

Food: seeds, insects, fruit; comes to seed feeders

Compare: Lacks the rusty crown of the American Tree Sparrow (pg. 97) and Chipping Sparrow (pg. 77). Look for the black bib of the male House Sparrow and the clear breast of the female House Sparrow.

Stan's Notes: One of the first bird songs heard in cities in spring. Familiar city bird, nearly always in small flocks. Introduced from Europe to Central Park in New York City in 1850. Now seen across North America. These birds are not really sparrows, but members of the Weaver Finch family, characterized by their large, oversized domed nests. Constructs a nest containing scraps of plastic, paper and whatever else is available. An aggressive bird that will kill the young of other birds in order to take over a cavity.

White-throated Sparrow
Zonotrichia albicollis

Size: 6-7" (15-18 cm)

Male: A brown bird with gray tan chest and belly. Small yellow spot between the eyes (lore). Distinctive white or tan throat patch. White or tan stripes alternate with black stripes on crown. Color of the throat patch and crown stripes match.

Female: same as male

Juvenile: similar to adult, gray throat and eyebrows with heavily streaked chest

Nest: cup; female builds; 1 brood per year

Eggs: 4-6; color varies from greenish to bluish to creamy white with red brown markings

Incubation: 11-14 days; female incubates

Fledging: 10-12 days; female and male feed young

Migration: complete, to Long Island, southern states

Food: insects, seeds, fruit; visits ground feeders

Compare: White-crowned Sparrow (pg. 103) lacks a throat patch and yellow lore.

Stan's Notes: Two color variations (polymorphic): white-striped and tan-striped. Studies indicate that the white-striped adults tend to mate with the tan-striped birds. No indication why. Known for its wonderful song. Sings all year and can even be heard at night. White- and tan-striped males and white-striped females sing, but tan-striped females do not. Builds nest on the ground under small trees in bogs and coniferous forests. Often associated with other sparrows during winter. Immature and first-year females tend to winter farther south than adults.

juvenile

White-crowned Sparrow

Zonotrichia leucophrys

WINTER

Size: 6½-7½" (16-19 cm)

Male: A brown sparrow with a gray breast and a black-and-white striped crown. Small, thin pink bill.

Female: same as male

Juvenile: similar to adult, with brown stripes on the head instead of white

Nest: cup; female builds; 2 broods per year

Eggs: 3-5; color varies from greenish to bluish to whitish with red brown markings

Incubation: 11-14 days; female incubates

Fledging: 8-12 days; male and female feed young

Migration: complete, to New York, southern states and Mexico

Food: insects, seeds, berries; visits ground feeders

Compare: White-throated Sparrow (pg. 101) has a white or tan throat patch and blackish bill, with a yellow spot between eyes and bill.

Stan's Notes: Usually seen in groups of up to 20 during migration, when it can be seen feeding under seed feeders. Males arrive before females and establish territories by singing from perches. A ground feeder, scratching backward with both feet at the same time. Male takes most of the responsibility of raising the young while female starts the second brood. Only 9-12 days separate the broods. Nests in Canada and Alaska.

CD 1, TRACK 50

Fox Sparrow
Passerella iliaca

MIGRATION
WINTER

Size: 7" (18 cm)

Male: A plump rusty red sparrow with a heavily streaked, rust-colored breast and solid rust tail. Head and back are mottled with gray.

Female: same as male

Juvenile: same as adult

Nest: cup; female builds; 2 broods per year

Eggs: 2-4; pale green with reddish markings

Incubation: 12-14 days; female incubates

Fledging: 10-11 days; female and male feed young

Migration: complete, to Long Island, southern states

Food: insects, seeds; comes to feeders

Compare: Similar coloration as the Brown Thrasher (pg. 131), but the Fox Sparrow is smaller, plumper and has a smaller bill. Rusty color differentiates it from all other sparrows.

Stan's Notes: One of the largest sparrows. Several color variations, depending upon the part of the country. Usually seen only under seed feeders during migration, searching for seeds and insects. Scratches like a chicken with both feet at the same time to find food. Usually alone or in small groups. Common name "Sparrow" comes from the Anglo-Saxon word *spearwa*, meaning "flutterer," as applied to any small bird. "Fox" refers to its rusty color. Nests on the ground in brush and along forest edges in Canada and Alaska.

male pg. 3

female

Eastern Towhee
Pipilo erythrophthalmus

Size: 7-8" (18-20 cm)

Female: A mostly light brown bird. Rusty red brown sides and white belly. Long brown tail with white tip. Short, stout, pointed bill and rich red eyes. White wing patches flash in flight.

Male: similar to female, but is black, not brown

Juvenile: light brown, a heavily streaked head, chest and belly, long dark tail with white tip

Nest: cup; female builds; 2 broods per year

Eggs: 3-4; creamy white with brown markings

Incubation: 12-13 days; female incubates

Fledging: 10-12 days; male and female feed young

Migration: complete, to southern states, Mexico and Central and South America

Food: insects, seeds, fruit; visits ground feeders

Compare: Slightly smaller than the American Robin (pg. 209), which has a red breast and lacks the white belly of the Eastern Towhee. The female Rose-breasted Grosbeak (pg. 115) has a heavily streaked breast and obvious white eyebrows.

Stan's Notes: Common name comes from its distinctive "tow-hee" call given by both sexes. Mostly known for its characteristic call that sounds like, "Drink-your-tea!" Seen hopping backward with both feet (bilateral scratching), raking up leaf litter for insects and seeds. The female broods, but male does the most feeding of young. In southern coastal states, some have red eyes; others have white eyes.

1 year old

Bohemian
Waxwing

Cedar Waxwing
Bombycilla cedrorum

YEAR-ROUND

Size: 7½" (19 cm)

Male: Very sleek-looking gray-to-brown bird with pointed crest, light yellow belly and bandit-like black mask. Tip of tail is bright yellow and the tips of wings look as if they have been dipped in red wax.

Female: same as male

Juvenile: grayish with a heavily streaked chest, lacks red wing tips, black mask and sleek look

Nest: cup; female and male construct; 1 brood per year, occasionally 2

Eggs: 4-6; pale blue with brown markings

Incubation: 10-12 days; female incubates

Fledging: 14-18 days; female and male feed young

Migration: partial migrator; moves around to find food

Food: cedar cones, fruit, insects

Compare: Similar to its larger, less common cousin, Bohemian Waxwing (see inset), which has white on wings and rust under tail. Female Cardinal (pg. 123) has a large red bill.

Stan's Notes: The name is derived from its red wax-like wing tips and preference for eating small blueberry-like cones of the cedar. Mostly seen in flocks, moving from area to area, looking for berries. Wanders in winter to find available food supplies. During summer, before berries are abundant, it feeds on insects. Spends most of its time at the tops of tall trees. Listen for the very high-pitched "sreee" whistling sounds it constantly makes. Obtains mask after first year and red wing tips after second year.

male pg. 5

female

YEAR-ROUND

Brown-headed Cowbird
Molothrus ater

Size: 7½" (19 cm)

Female: Dull brown bird with no obvious markings. Pointed, sharp gray bill.

Male: glossy black bird, chocolate brown head

Juvenile: similar to female, only dull gray color and a streaked chest

Nest: no nest; lays eggs in nests of other birds

Eggs: 5-7; white with brown markings

Incubation: 10-13 days; host bird incubates eggs

Fledging: 10-11 days; host birds feed young

Migration: non-migrator in New York

Food: insects, seeds; will come to seed feeders

Compare: Female Red-winged Blackbird (pg. 125) is slightly larger and has white eyebrows and a streaked chest. European Starling (pg. 7) has speckles and a shorter tail.

Stan's Notes: A member of the blackbird family. Of approximately 750 species of parasitic birds worldwide, this is the only parasitic bird in New York, laying eggs in host birds' nests, leaving others to raise its young. Cowbirds are known to have laid eggs in nests of over 200 species of birds. Some birds reject cowbird eggs, but most incubate them and raise the young, even to the exclusion of their own. Look for warblers and other birds feeding young birds twice their own size. At one time cowbirds followed bison to feed on insects attracted to the animals.

Horned Lark
Eremophila alpestris

YEAR-ROUND
WINTER

Size: 7-8" (18-20 cm)

Male: A sleek tan-to-brown bird. Black necklace with a yellow chin and black bill. Two tiny "horns" on the top of head can be difficult to see. A dark tail with white outer feathers, noticeable in flight.

Female: duller than male, "horns" less noticeable

Juvenile: lacks the black markings and yellow chin, doesn't form "horns" until second year

Nest: ground; female builds; 2-3 broods per year

Eggs: 3-4; gray with brown markings

Incubation: 11-12 days; female incubates

Fledging: 9-12 days; female and male feed young

Migration: non-migrator to partial in New York

Food: seeds, insects

Compare: Smaller than Meadowlark (pg. 293), which shares the black necklace and yellow chin. Look for the black marks in front of eyes.

Stan's Notes: The only true lark native to North America. Moves around during winter to find food. Horned Larks are birds of open ground. Common in rural areas, frequently seen in large flocks. Population increased in North America over the past 100 years due to land clearing for farming. May have up to three broods per year because they get such an early start. Male performs a fluttering courtship flight high in the air while singing a high-pitched song. Female performs a fluttering distraction display if nest is disturbed. Can renest about a week after brood fledges. The name "Lark" comes from the Middle English word *laverock*, or "a lark."

female

male pg. 27

SUMMER

Rose-breasted Grosbeak
Pheucticus ludovicianus

Size: 7-8" (18-20 cm)

Female: Plump, heavily streaked brown and white bird with obvious white eyebrows. Orange yellow wing linings.

Male: black-and-white bird with large, triangular rose patch in center of chest, wing linings are rosy red

Juvenile: similar to female

Nest: cup; female and male construct; 1-2 broods per year

Eggs: 3-5; blue green with brown markings

Incubation: 13-14 days; female and male incubate

Fledging: 9-12 days; female and male feed young

Migration: complete, to Mexico, Central America and South America

Food: insects, seeds, fruit; comes to seed feeders

Compare: Looks like a large sparrow. Larger and has a more distinctive eyebrow mark than female Purple Finch (pg. 95). Female House Finch (pg. 81) lacks the eyebrow mark.

Stan's Notes: Usually prefers mature deciduous forest for nesting. Both sexes sing, but the male sings much louder and clearer. Has a rich, robin-like song. "Grosbeak" refers to its large bill, used to crush seeds. Late to arrive in spring; early to leave in fall. Males arrive in small groups first, joined by females several days later. Several males can be seen visiting seed feeders at the same time in spring. When females arrive, males become territorial and reduce their visits to feeders. Young grosbeaks visit feeders with adults after fledging.

winter

breeding

Spotted Sandpiper
Actitis macularius

Size: 8" (20 cm)

Male: Olive brown back. Long bill and long dull yellow legs. White line over eyes. Breeding plumage has black spots on a white chest and belly. Winter has a clear chest and belly.

Female: same as male

Juvenile: similar to winter adult, with a darker bill

Nest: ground; female and male build; 2 broods per year

Eggs: 3-4; brownish with brown markings

Incubation: 20-24 days; male incubates

Fledging: 17-21 days; male feeds young

Migration: complete, to southern states, Mexico and Central and South America

Food: aquatic insects

Compare: Smaller than Lesser Yellowlegs (pg. 129). Look for Spotted Sandpiper to bob its tail up and down while standing. Look for the breeding Spotted Sandpiper's black spots extending from chest to belly.

Stan's Notes: One of the few shorebirds that will dive underwater if pursued. Able to fly straight up out of the water. Flies with wings held in a cup-like arc, rarely lifting them above a horizontal plane. Constantly bobs its tail while standing and walks as if delicately balanced. Female mates with multiple males and lays eggs in up to five different nests. Male incubates and cares for young. Dramatic plumage change from breeding to winter. Lacks black spots on the chest and belly in winter.

 **CD 1, TRACK 54**

winter pg. 197

breeding

Sanderling
Calidris alba

MIGRATION
WINTER

Size: 8" (20 cm)

Male: Breeding has a rusty head, breast and back with a white belly. Black legs and bill.

Female: same as male

Juvenile: spotty black on the head and back, a white belly, black legs and bill

Nest: ground; male builds; 1-2 broods per year

Eggs: 3-4; greenish olive with brown markings

Incubation: 24-30 days; male and female incubate

Fledging: 16-17 days; female and male feed young

Migration: complete, to the East and Gulf coasts, West Indies, Mexico, Central and South America

Food: insects

Compare: Spotted Sandpiper (pg. 117) is the same size as Sanderling, but the breeding Spotted Sandpiper has black spots on its chest.

Stan's Notes: Very common shorebird in New York. Can be seen in groups on sandy beaches, running out with each retreating wave to feed. Look for flash of white on wings when it is in flight. Sometimes a female will mate with several males (polyandry), which results in males and the female incubating separate nests. Both sexes perform distraction displays if threatened. Stands on one leg to rest and tucks the other into its belly feathers. Often hops on one leg, moving away from pedestrians on beaches. Surveys show population declines of greater than 80 percent since the 1970s. Nests on the Arctic tundra. Seen in breeding plumage from April to August.

winter
pg. 199

breeding

Dunlin
Calidris alpina

Size: 8-9" (20-22.5 cm)

Male: Breeding adult is distinctive with a rusty red back, finely streaked chest and an obvious black patch on the belly. Stout bill, curving slightly downward at the tip. Black legs.

Female: slightly larger than male, with a longer bill

Juvenile: slightly rusty back with a spotty chest

Nest: ground; male and female construct; 1 brood per year

Eggs: 2-4; olive buff or blue green with red brown markings

Incubation: 21-22 days; male and female incubate, male incubates during the day, female at night

Fledging: 19-21 days; male feeds young, female often leaves before young fledge

Migration: complete, to Long Island, the East and Gulf coasts, Mexico and Central America

Food: insects

Compare: Similar in size to the breeding Sanderling (pg. 119), look for the obvious black belly patch and curved bill of breeding Dunlin.

Stan's Notes: Flights include heights of up to 100 feet (30 m) with brief gliding alternating with shallow flutters, and a rhythmic, repeating song. Huge flocks fly synchronously, with birds twisting and turning, flashing light and dark undersides. Males tend to fly farther south in winter than females. Winter visitor in Long Island. Doesn't nest in New York.

CD 1, TRACK 56

male pg. 255

female

juvenile

YEAR-ROUND

Northern Cardinal
Cardinalis cardinalis

Size: 8-9" (20-22.5 cm)

Female: Buff brown bird with tinges of red on crest and wings, a black mask and large red bill.

Male: red bird with a black mask extending from face down to chin and throat, large red bill and crest

Juvenile: same as female, but with a blackish gray bill

Nest: cup; female builds; 2-3 broods per year

Eggs: 3-4; bluish white with brown markings

Incubation: 12-13 days; female and male incubate

Fledging: 9-10 days; female and male feed young

Migration: non-migrator

Food: seeds, insects, fruit; comes to seed feeders

Compare: The male Red Crossbill (pg. 251) has dark brown wings and a thinner crossed bill. The Cedar Waxwing (pg. 109) has a small dark bill. The female Northern Cardinal appears similar to juvenile Cardinal, but the juvenile has a dark bill. Look for the bright red bill of female Cardinal.

Stan's Notes: A familiar backyard bird. Look for the male feeding female during courtship. Male feeds young of the first brood by himself while female builds second nest. The name comes from the Latin word *cardinalis*, which means "important." Very territorial in spring, it will fight its own reflection in a window. Non-territorial during winter, gathering in small flocks of up to 20 birds. Both the female and male sing and can be heard anytime of year. Listen for its "whata-cheer-cheer-cheer" territorial call in spring.

 CD 1, TRACK 57

female

male pg. 9

Red-winged Blackbird
Agelaius phoeniceus

Size: 8½" (22 cm)

Female: Heavily streaked brown bird with a pointed brown bill and white eyebrows.

Male: jet black bird with red and yellow patches on upper wings, pointed black bill

Juvenile: same as female

Nest: cup; female builds; 2-3 broods per year

Eggs: 3-4; bluish green with brown markings

Incubation: 10-12 days; female incubates

Fledging: 11-14 days; female and male feed young

Migration: partial to non-migrator in New York

Food: seeds, insects; will come to seed feeders

Compare: Female Brown-headed Cowbird (pg. 111) lacks the white eyebrows and a heavily streaked breast. Similar to the female Rose-breasted Grosbeak (pg. 115), but female Red-winged Blackbird has a thinner body and pointed bill.

Stan's Notes: One of the most widespread and numerous birds in New York. It is a sure sign of spring when Red-winged Blackbirds return to the marshes. Flocks of up to 100,000 birds have been reported. Males return before the females and defend territories by singing from tops of surrounding vegetation. Males repeat call from the tops of cattails while showing off their red and yellow wing bars (epaulets). Females choose a mate and will often nest over shallow water in thick stands of cattails. Red-wingeds feed mostly on seeds in fall and spring, switching to insects during summer.

female

male

Common Nighthawk
Chordeiles minor

Size: 9" (22.5 cm)

Male: A camouflaged brown and white bird with white chin. A distinctive white band across wings and the tail, seen only in flight.

Female: similar to male, but with a tan chin, lacks a white tail band

Juvenile: similar to female

Nest: no nest; lays eggs on the ground, usually on rocks, or on rooftop; 1 brood per year

Eggs: 2; cream with lavender markings

Incubation: 19-20 days; female and male incubate

Fledging: 20-21 days; female and male feed young

Migration: complete, to South America

Food: insects caught in air

Compare: Much larger than Chimney Swift (pg. 75). Look for the obvious white wing band of the Nighthawk in flight and characteristic flap-flap-flap-glide flight pattern.

Stan's Notes: Usually only seen flying at dusk or after sunset, but not uncommon for it to be sitting on a fence post, sleeping during the day. A very noisy bird, repeating a "peenting" call during flight. Alternates slow wing beats with bursts of quick wing beats. Prolific insect eater. Prefers gravel rooftops for nesting in cities and nests on the ground in country. Male's distinctive springtime mating ritual is a steep diving flight terminated with a loud popping noise. One of the first birds to migrate each fall, starting in August.

MIGRATION

Lesser Yellowlegs
Tringa flavipes

Size: 10-11" (25-28 cm)

Male: A typical sandpiper-type bird with a brown back and wings and lightly streaked white breast and belly. Thin, straight black bill. Long yellow legs.

Female: same as male

Juvenile: same as adult

Nest: ground; female builds; 1 brood per year

Eggs: 3-4; yellowish with brown markings

Incubation: 22-23 days; male and female incubate

Fledging: 18-20 days; male and female lead young to food

Migration: complete, to southern coastal states, South America

Food: aquatic insects, tiny fish

Compare: Very similar to Greater Yellowlegs (pg. 143), but has a shorter bill. The breeding Spotted Sandpiper (pg. 117) has spots on its chest.

Stan's Notes: Usually seen in small flocks, it combs shorelines and mud flats looking for aquatic insects. Most often seen in the head down, tail up position, walking along, looking to snatch up food. Uses its long straight bill to pluck insects and tiny fish from water. Very shy bird that quite often moves into the water prior to taking flight. Has a variety of "flight" notes that it gives when taking off. A member of the group of sandpipers called Tattlers, all of which scream alarm calls when taking flight. Nests on marshes in spruce forests of central Alaska and central Canada. Migrates later than the Greater Yellowlegs in spring and earlier in fall.

Brown Thrasher
Toxostoma rufum

Size: 11" (28 cm)

Male: A rusty red bird with long tail and heavily streaked breast and belly. Two white wing bars. Long curved bill. Bright yellow eyes.

Female: same as male

Juvenile: same as adult, but eye color is grayish

Nest: cup; female and male construct; 2 broods per year

Eggs: 4-5; pale blue with brown markings

Incubation: 11-14 days; female and male incubate

Fledging: 10-13 days; female and male feed young

Migration: complete, to southern states

Food: insects, fruit

Compare: Slightly larger in size and similar in shape to the American Robin (pg. 209) and Gray Catbird (pg. 205), but the Brown Thrasher is rusty with a streaked breast and yellow eyes. Similar rust color as the Fox Sparrow (pg. 105), but the Brown Thrasher is larger and thinner.

Stan's Notes: A prodigious songster, often in thick shrubs where it sings deliberate musical phrases, repeating each twice. Male has the largest documented song repertoire of all North American birds, with over 1,100 song types. Often seen quickly flying or running in and out of dense shrubs. Noisy feeding due to habit of turning over leaves, small rocks and branches. This bird is more abundant in the central Great Plains than anywhere else in North America.

CD 2, TRACK 3

YEAR-ROUND
SUMMER

Killdeer
Charadrius vociferus

Size: 11" (28 cm)

Male: An upland shorebird that has 2 black bands around the neck like a necklace. A brown back and white belly. Bright reddish orange rump, visible in flight.

Female: same as male

Juvenile: similar to adult, with 1 neck band

Nest: ground; male builds; 2 broods per year

Eggs: 3-5; tan with brown markings

Incubation: 24-28 days; male and female incubate

Fledging: 25 days; male and female lead their young to food

Migration: complete, to southern states, Mexico and Central America

Food: insects

Compare: The Spotted Sandpiper (pg. 117) is found around water and lacks the 2 neck bands of the Killdeer.

Stan's Notes: The only shorebird with two black neck bands. It is known for its broken wing impression, which draws intruders away from nest. Once clear of the nest, the Killdeer takes flight. Nests are only a slight depression in a gravel area, often very difficult to see. Young look like miniature adults on stilts when first hatched. Able to follow parents and peck for insects soon after birth. Is technically classified as a shorebird, but doesn't live at the shore. Often found in vacant fields or along railroads. Has a very distinctive "kill-deer" call.

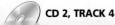 **CD 2, TRACK 4**

American Kestrel
Falco sparverius

Size: 10-12" (25-30 cm); up to 2-foot wingspan

Male: Rusty brown back and tail. A white breast with dark spots. Double black vertical lines on white face. Blue gray wings. Distinctive wide black band with a white edge on tip of rusty tail.

Female: similar to male, but slightly larger, has rusty brown wings and dark bands on tail

Juvenile: same as adult of the same sex

Nest: cavity; doesn't build a nest within; 1 brood per year

Eggs: 4-5; white with brown markings

Incubation: 29-31 days; male and female incubate

Fledging: 30-31 days; female and male feed young

Migration: complete; small percentage will not migrate

Food: insects, small mammals and birds, reptiles

Compare: Similar to other falcons. Look for 2 vertical black stripes on the Kestrel's face. No other small bird of prey has a rusty back and tail.

Stan's Notes: A falcon that was once called Sparrow Hawk due to its small size. Could be called Grasshopper Hawk because it eats many grasshoppers. Can see ultraviolet light; this ability helps it locate mice and other small mammals by their urine, which glows bright yellow in ultraviolet light. Hovers near roads before diving for prey. Adapts quickly to a wooden nest box. Has pointed swept-back wings, seen in flight. Perches nearly upright. Unusual raptor in that males and females have quite different markings. Watch for them to pump their tails up and down after landing on perches.

male

female

Northern Flicker
Colaptes auratus

YEAR-ROUND

Size: 12" (30 cm)

Male: Brown and black woodpecker with a large white rump patch visible only when flying. Black necklace above a speckled breast. Red spot on nape of neck. Black mustache.

Female: same as male, but lacks a black mustache

Juvenile: same as adult of the same sex

Nest: cavity; female and male excavate; 1 brood per year

Eggs: 5-8; white without markings

Incubation: 11-14 days; female and male incubate

Fledging: 25-28 days; female and male feed young

Migration: non-migrator in New York

Food: insects, especially ants and beetles

Compare: The male Yellow-bellied Sapsucker (pg. 29) is smaller and has a red chin and forehead. The male Red-bellied Woodpecker (pg. 35) has a red crown, a black-and-white zebra-striped back and lacks a mustache. Flickers are the only brown-backed woodpeckers in New York.

Stan's Notes: This is the only woodpecker to regularly feed on the ground. Preferring ants and beetles, it produces an antacid saliva to neutralize the acid defense of ants. Male usually selects a nest site, taking up to 12 days to excavate. Some have had success attracting flickers to nest boxes stuffed with sawdust. In flight, it undulates deeply, flashes golden yellow under wings and tail and calls "wacka-wacka" loudly. Populations swell in winter with northern migrants.

CD 2, TRACK 6

YEAR-ROUND

Mourning Dove
Zenaida macroura

Size: 12" (30 cm)

Male: Smooth fawn-colored dove with gray patch on the head. Iridescent pink, green around neck. A single black spot behind and below eyes. Black spots on wings and tail. Pointed wedge-shaped tail with white edges.

Female: similar to male, lacking iridescent pink and green neck feathers

Juvenile: spotted and streaked

Nest: platform; female and male build; 2 broods per year

Eggs: 2; white without markings

Incubation: 13-14 days; male and female incubate, male incubates during the day, female at night

Fledging: 12-14 days; female and male feed young

Migration: non-migrator to partial, to southern states; will move around to find food

Food: seeds; will visit seed and ground feeders

Compare: Smaller than Rock Pigeon (pg. 217), lacking its wide range of color combinations.

Stan's Notes: Name comes from its mournful cooing. A ground feeder, bobbing its head as it walks. One of the few birds to drink without lifting its head, same as Rock Pigeon. Parents feed young (squab) a regurgitated liquid called crop-milk the first few days of life. Flimsy platform nest of twigs often falls apart in storms. Wind rushing through wing feathers during flight creates a characteristic whistling sound.

CD 2, TRACK 7

winter

breeding

Pied-billed Grebe
Podilymbus podiceps

SUMMER
WINTER

Size: 13" (33 cm)

Male: Small brown water bird with a black chin and black ring around a thick, chicken-like ivory bill. Puffy white patch under the tail. Has an unmarked brown bill during winter.

Female: same as male

Juvenile: paler than adult, with white spots and gray chest, belly and bill

Nest: floating platform; female and male build; 1 brood per year

Eggs: 5-7; bluish white without markings

Incubation: 22-24 days; female and male incubate

Fledging: 22-24 days; female and male feed young

Migration: complete, to Long Island, southern states, Mexico and Central America

Food: crayfish, aquatic insects, fish

Compare: Look for a puffy white patch under the tail and thick, chicken-like bill to help identify.

Stan's Notes: Very common water bird, often seen diving for food. Slowly sinks like a submarine when disturbed. Sinks without diving by quickly compressing feathers to force air out. Was called Hell-diver because of length of time it can stay submerged. Can surface far from where it went under. Very sensitive to pollution. Well suited to life on water, with short wings, lobed toes, and legs set close to rear of its body. While swimming is easy, it is very awkward on land. Builds nest on a floating mat in water. "Grebe" probably came from the Old English word *krib*, meaning "crest," a reference to the crested head plumes of many grebes, especially during breeding season.

Greater Yellowlegs
Tringa melanoleuca

MIGRATION

Size: 14" (36 cm)

Male: Tall bird with a bulbous head and long thin bill, slightly upturned. Gray streaking on chest. White belly. Long yellow legs.

Female: same as male

Juvenile: same as adult

Nest: ground; female builds; 1 brood per year

Eggs: 3-4; off-white with brown markings

Incubation: 22-23 days; female and male incubate

Fledging: 18-20 days; male and female feed young

Migration: complete, to southern states, Mexico and Central and South America

Food: small fish, aquatic insects

Compare: The Lesser Yellowlegs (pg. 129) is smaller and has a shorter, straight bill unlike the long upturned bill of Greater Yellowlegs.

Stan's Notes: A common shorebird that can be identified by the slightly upturned bill and long yellow legs. Often seen resting on one leg. Its long legs carry it through deep water. Feeds by rushing forward through the water, plowing its bill or swinging it from side to side, catching small fish and insects. A skittish bird quick to give an alarm call, causing flocks to take flight. Quite often moves into the water prior to taking flight. Has a variety of "flight" notes that it gives when taking off. Nests on the ground close to water on the northern tundra of Labrador and Newfoundland.

male

female

Blue-winged Teal
Anas discors

MIGRATION
SUMMER

Size: 15-16" (38-40 cm)

Male: Small, plain-looking brown duck speckled with black. A gray head with a large white crescent-shaped mark at base of bill. Black tail with small white patch. Blue wing patch (speculum), usually seen only in flight.

Female: duller than male, lacks white patch on tail, has only slight white at base of bill

Juvenile: same as female

Nest: ground; female builds; 1 brood per year

Eggs: 8-11; creamy white

Incubation: 23-27 days; female incubates

Fledging: 35-44 days; female feeds young

Migration: complete, to southern states, Mexico and Central America

Food: aquatic plants, seeds, aquatic insects

Compare: Male Blue-winged Teal has a distinct white mark at the base of bill. Female Wood Duck (pg. 155) and Mallard (pg. 171) are larger than the female Blue-winged Teal, and the Wood Duck has a crest.

Stan's Notes: This is one of the smallest ducks in North America. A widespread nester that breeds as far north as Alaska. One of the longest distance migrating ducks and common migrant in the state. Constructs its nest some distance from the water. Female performs a distraction display to protect nest and young. Male leaves female near the end of incubation. Planting crops and cultivating to pond edges have caused a decline in population.

CD 2, TRACK 10

male pg. 39

female

WINTER

Lesser Scaup
Aythya affinis

Size: 16-17" (40-43 cm)

Female: Overall brown duck with dull white patch at base of light gray bill. Yellow eyes.

Male: white and gray, the chest and head appear nearly black but head appears purple with green highlights in direct sun, yellow eyes

Juvenile: same as female

Nest: ground; female builds; 1 brood per year

Eggs: 8-14; olive buff without markings

Incubation: 22-28 days; female incubates

Fledging: 45-50 days; female teaches young to feed

Migration: complete, to New York and southern states

Food: aquatic plants and insects

Compare: Male Blue-winged Teal (pg. 145) is slightly smaller and has a crescent-shaped white mark at the base of bill. The female Wood Duck (pg. 155) is larger with white around the eyes.

Stan's Notes: A common diving duck. Often in large flocks along western Lake Erie each spring. Mostly seen when it migrates in late February and October. Submerges to feed on the bottom of lakes (unlike dabbling ducks, which tip forward to reach bottom). Note the bold white stripe under wings when in flight. Male leaves female when she starts to incubate her eggs. Quantity of eggs (clutch size) increases with age of female. Interesting baby-sitting arrangement in which groups of young (crèches) are tended by 1-3 adult females.

soaring

Broad-winged Hawk
Buteo platypterus

Size: 14-19" (36-48 cm); up to 3-foot wingspan

Male: A hawk slightly smaller than the American Crow, the Broad-winged has a brown back and rusty red barring on chest. Tail has 2-3 wide black-and-white bands. White under wings with black "fingertips," seen in flight.

Female: same as male

Juvenile: tail bands narrower and more numerous, a brown-streaked chest and belly

Nest: platform; female and male build, but female finishes; 1 brood per year

Eggs: 2-3; off-white with brown markings

Incubation: 28-32 days; female incubates, male feeds the female during incubation

Fledging: 34-35 days; female and male feed young

Migration: complete, to Central and South America

Food: small mammals, small birds, large insects, snakes, frogs

Compare: Similar in size to Cooper's Hawk (pg. 221), but with a wider, shorter tail. Larger than Sharp-shinned Hawk (pg. 219). Look for the alternating black-and-white tail bands.

Stan's Notes: A very common woodland hawk in New York. Often seen in large groups (kettles) migrating early in autumn. Massive migration provides a spectacular sight along the Great Lakes shoreline. Spends most of its time hunting small birds, snakes and frogs in dense woodlands. Short round wings propel it through dense woods. Screams "call" repetitively when intruders are near the nest.

drumming

YEAR-ROUND

Ruffed Grouse
Bonasa umbellus

Size: 16-19" (40-48 cm); up to 2-foot wingspan

Male: Brown chicken-like bird with long squared tail. Wide black band near tip of tail. Is able to fan tail like a turkey. Tuft of feathers on the head stands like a crown. Black ruffs on sides of neck.

Female: same as male, but less obvious neck ruffs

Juvenile: same as female

Nest: ground; female builds; 1 brood per year

Eggs: 9-12; tan with light brown markings

Incubation: 23-24 days; female incubates

Fledging: 10-12 days; female leads young to food

Migration: non-migrator

Food: seeds, insects, fruit, leaf buds

Compare: Female Ring-necked Pheasant (pg. 173) is larger with a longer, pointed tail. Look for a feathered tuft on the head and black ruffs on the neck of the Ruffed Grouse.

Stan's Notes: A common bird of deep forests. Often seen in aspen or other trees, feeding on leaf buds. During winter in the more northern climates, it grows bristles on its feet, which serve as snowshoes. If there is enough snow, it will dive into a snowbank to roost at night. During spring, male raises its crest (tuft), fans tail feathers, stands on logs and drums with wings to attract females. Drumming sound comes from cupped wings moving air, not pounding on its chest or a log. Female performs a distraction display to protect her young. Two color morphs, red and gray, most apparent in the tail. Black ruffs around the neck gave rise to its common name.

male pg. 41

female

Hooded Merganser
Lophodytes cucullatus

MIGRATION WINTER

Size: 16-19" (40-48 cm)

Female: Sleek brown and rust bird with a red head. Ragged "hair" on back of head. Long, thin brown bill.

Male: same size and shape as female, but a black back and rust sides, crest "hood" raises to reveal large white patch, long black bill

Juvenile: similar to female

Nest: cavity; female lines old woodpecker hole; 1 brood per year

Eggs: 10-12; white without markings

Incubation: 32-33 days; female incubates

Fledging: 71 days; female feeds young

Migration: complete, to Long Island, southern states

Food: small fish, aquatic insects

Compare: Smaller than female Common Merganser (pg. 259), which has a white chin and large orange bill. Larger than female Lesser Scaup (pg. 147), which has a dull white patch at base of bill.

Stan's Notes: A small diving bird of shallow ponds, sloughs, lakes and rivers. Male Hooded Merganser can voluntarily raise and lower its crest to show off the large white head patch. Rarely found away from wooded areas, where it nests in natural cavities or nest boxes. Female will "dump" her eggs into other female Hooded Merganser nests, resulting in 20-25 eggs in some nests. Known to share nest cavities with Common Goldeneyes and Wood Ducks, sitting side by side. Not as common as the Common Merganser.

male pg. 231

female

SUMMER

Wood Duck
Aix sponsa

Size: 17-20" (43-50 cm)

Female: A small brown dabbling duck. Bright white eye-ring and a not-so-obvious crest. A blue patch on wing, often hidden.

Male: highly ornamented with a green head and crest patterned with white and black, rusty chest, white belly and red eyes

Juvenile: same as female

Nest: cavity; female lines old woodpecker cavity; 1 brood per year

Eggs: 10-15; creamy white without markings

Incubation: 28-36 days; female incubates

Fledging: 56-68 days; female teaches young to feed

Migration: complete, to southern states

Food: aquatic insects, plants, seeds

Compare: Female Mallard (pg. 171) and female Blue-winged Teal (pg. 145) lack the bright white eye-ring and crest. The female Northern Shoveler (pg. 159) is larger and has a large spoon-shaped bill.

Stan's Notes: A common duck of quiet, shallow backwater ponds. Nests in old woodpecker holes or in nest boxes. Often seen flying deep in forests or perched high on tree branches. Female takes to flight with a loud squealing call, entering nest cavity from full flight. Will lay eggs in a neighboring female nest (egg dumping), resulting in some clutches in excess of 20 eggs. Young stay in nest cavity only 24 hours after hatching, then jump from up to 30 feet (9 m) to the ground or water to follow their mother, never returning to the nest.

 CD 2, TRACK 13

female

male pg. 47

Common Goldeneye
Bucephala clangula

MIGRATION
SUMMER
WINTER

Size: 18½-20" (47-50 cm)

Female: A brown and gray duck with a large dark brown head and gray body. White collar. Bright golden eyes. Yellow-tipped dark bill.

Male: mostly white duck with a black back and a large, puffy green head, large white spot in front of each bright golden eye, dark bill

Juvenile: same as female, but has a dark bill

Nest: cavity; female lines old woodpecker cavity; 1 brood per year

Eggs: 8-10; light green without markings

Incubation: 28-32 days; female incubates

Fledging: 56-59 days; female leads young to food

Migration: complete, to New York, southern states and Mexico

Food: aquatic plants, insects

Compare: Similar to female Lesser Scaup (pg. 147), which is smaller. Look for the female Common Goldeneye's dark brown head and white collar.

Stan's Notes: Known for its loud whistling, produced by its wings in flight. In late winter and early spring, male often attracts female through elaborate displays, throwing its head backward while it utters a single raspy note. Female will lay eggs in other goldeneye nests, which results in some mothers incubating up to 30 eggs. Received the common name from its obvious bright golden eyes. Winters in parts of New York where it finds open water.

male pg. 235

female

Northern Shoveler

Anas clypeata

Size: 20" (50 cm)

Female: Medium-sized brown duck speckled with black. Green speculum. An extraordinarily large spoon-shaped bill, almost always held pointed toward the water.

Male: iridescent green head, rusty sides and white breast, spoon-shaped bill

Juvenile: same as female

Nest: ground; female builds; 1 brood per year

Eggs: 9-12; olive without markings

Incubation: 22-25 days; female incubates

Fledging: 30-60 days; female leads young to food

Migration: complete, to New York, southern states, Mexico and Central America

Food: aquatic insects, plants

Compare: Similar color as female Mallard (pg. 171), but Mallard lacks the Shoveler's large bill. Female Wood Duck (pg. 155) is smaller and has a white eye-ring. Look for the Shoveler's large spoon-shaped bill to help identify.

Stan's Notes: One of several species of shoveler, so called because of the peculiar shape of its bill. The Northern Shoveler is the only species of these ducks in North America. Found in small flocks of 5-10, swimming low in water with its large bill pointed toward the water, as if it's too heavy to lift. Feeds mainly by filtering tiny aquatic insects and plants from the water's surface with its bill.

YEAR-ROUND

Barred Owl
Strix varia

Size: 20-24" (50-60 cm); up to 3½-foot wingspan

Male: A chunky brown and gray owl with a large head and dark brown eyes. Dark horizontal barring on upper chest. Vertical streaks on lower chest and belly. Yellow bill and feet.

Female: same as male, only slightly larger

Juvenile: light gray with a black face

Nest: cavity; does not add any nesting material; 1 brood per year

Eggs: 2-3; white without markings

Incubation: 28-33 days; female incubates

Fledging: 42-44 days; female and male feed young

Migration: non-migrator

Food: mammals, birds, fish, reptiles, amphibians

Compare: Lacks the "horns" of the Great Horned Owl (pg. 167) and ear tufts of the tiny Eastern Screech-Owl (pg. 207). Eastern Screech-Owl is less than half the size of Barred Owl.

Stan's Notes: A very common owl that can often be seen hunting during the day, perching and watching for mice, birds and other prey. One of the few owls to take fish out of a lake. Prefers dense deciduous woodlands with sparse undergrowth. Can be attracted with a simple nest box with a large opening, attached to a tree. The young stay with their parents for up to four months after fledging. Often sounds like a dog barking just before giving an eight-hoot call that sounds like, "Who-cooks-for-you? Who-cooks-for-you?" The Great Horned Owl sounds like, "Hoo-hoo-hoo-hoooo!"

male

female

American Black Duck
Anas rubripes

Size: 22" (56 cm)

Male: Overall dark brown, sometimes appearing nearly black, with a lighter head and neck. A yellow bill and orange legs. Violet patch on the wings (speculum), bordered with black. Dark wings contrast sharply with white wing linings, seen in flight.

Female: same as male, except bill is dull green with black flecks

Juvenile: same as female

Nest: ground; female builds; 1 brood per year

Eggs: 8-10; creamy white to greenish buff

Incubation: 26-29 days; female incubates

Fledging: 16-17 days; female teaches young to feed

Migration: non-migrator to partial in New York

Food: aquatic plants, seeds

Compare: Male and female American Black Ducks are very similar to the female Mallard (pg. 171), but the female Mallard has an orange bill and a blue wing patch (speculum) bordered with white.

Stan's Notes: Was once one of the most abundant ducks breeding in the U.S. Mallards are more common now. Sometimes hybridizes (mates) with Mallards, producing a bird lacking the brilliant colors of the male Mallard. Female constructs a nest in grass that is high enough to conceal. Male leaves female while she is still incubating eggs. Young leave the nest 1-3 hours after hatching.

soaring

YEAR-ROUND

Red-tailed Hawk
Buteo jamaicensis

Size: 19-25" (48-63 cm); up to 4-foot wingspan

Male: Large hawk with amazing variety of colors from bird to bird, from chocolate brown to nearly all white. Often brown with a white breast and a distinctive brown belly band. Rust red tail, usually seen only from above. Wing underside is white with a small dark patch on leading edge near shoulder.

Female: same as male, only slightly larger

Juvenile: similar to adults, lacking the red tail, has a speckled chest and light eyes

Nest: platform; male and female build; 1 brood per year

Eggs: 2-3; white without markings or sometimes marked with brown

Incubation: 30-35 days; female and male incubate

Fledging: 45-46 days; male and female feed young

Migration: partial to non-migrator

Food: mice, birds, snakes, insects, mammals

Compare: Broad-winged Hawk (pg. 149), Cooper's Hawk (pg. 221) and Sharp-shinned Hawk (pg. 219) are smaller and lack the red tail.

Stan's Notes: A common hawk of open country and in cities, often seen perched on freeway light posts, fences and trees. Look for it circling over open fields and roadsides, searching for prey. Their large stick nests are commonly seen in large trees along roads. Nests are lined with finer material such as evergreen tree needles. Returns to the same nest site each year. Develops red tail in the second year.

Great Horned Owl
Bubo virginianus

YEAR-ROUND

Size: 20-25" (50-63 cm); up to 3½-foot wingspan

Male: Robust brown "horned" owl. Bright yellow eyes and V-shaped white throat resembling a necklace. Horizontal barring on the chest.

Female: same as male, only slightly larger

Juvenile: similar to adults, lacking ear tufts

Nest: no nest; takes over the nest of a crow, Great Blue Heron or hawk or uses a partial cavity, stump or broken-off tree; 1 brood per year

Eggs: 2; white without markings

Incubation: 26-30 days; female incubates

Fledging: 30-35 days; male and female feed young

Migration: non-migrator

Food: mammals, birds (ducks), snakes, insects

Compare: Barred Owl (pg. 161) has dark eyes and no "horns." Over twice the size of its cousin, Eastern Screech-Owl (pg. 207). Look for bright yellow eyes and feathers on head that look like horns to help identify this bird.

Stan's Notes: One of the earliest nesting birds in the state, laying eggs in January and February. Has excellent hearing; able to hear a mouse moving beneath a foot of snow. "Ears" are actually tufts of feathers (horns) and have nothing to do with hearing. Not able to turn its head all the way around. Wing feathers are ragged on ends, resulting in a silent flight. The eyelids close from the top down, like humans. Fearless, it is one of the few animals that will kill skunks and porcupines. Because of this, it is sometimes called Flying Tiger.

male
pg. 223

female

soaring

Northern Harrier
Circus cyaneus

YEAR-ROUND
SUMMER

Size: 22½" (57 cm); up to 3½-foot wingspan

Female: A slim, low-flying hawk. Dark brown back with brown-streaked breast and belly. Large white rump patch and narrow black bands across tail. Black wing tips. Yellow eyes.

Male: silver gray with large white rump patch and white belly, faint narrow bands across tail, black wing tips, yellow eyes

Juvenile: similar to female, with an orange breast

Nest: platform, often on ground; female and male build; 1 brood per year

Eggs: 4-8; bluish white without markings

Incubation: 31-32 days; female incubates

Fledging: 30-35 days; male and female feed young

Migration: partial to non-migrator in New York

Food: mice, snakes, insects, small birds

Compare: Slimmer than Red-tailed Hawk (pg. 165). Look for black tail bands, white rump patch and characteristic flight to help identify.

Stan's Notes: One of the easiest hawks to identify. Harriers glide just above ground, following contours of the land while searching for prey. Holds its wings just above the horizontal position, tilting back and forth in the wind, similar to Turkey Vultures. Formerly called Marsh Hawk due to its habit of hunting over marshes. Feeds on the ground. Will perch on the ground to preen and rest. At any age, has a distinctive owl-like face disk.

male pg. 239

female

Mallard
Anas platyrhynchos

Size: 23" (58 cm)

Female: Brown duck with an orange and black bill and blue and white wing mark (speculum).

Male: large, bulbous green head, white necklace, rust brown or chestnut chest, combination of gray and white on the sides, yellow bill, orange legs and feet

Juvenile: same as female, but with a yellow bill

Nest: ground; female builds; 1 brood per year

Eggs: 7-10; greenish to whitish, unmarked

Incubation: 26-30 days; female incubates

Fledging: 42-52 days; female leads young to food

Migration: non-migrator to partial in New York

Food: seeds, plants, aquatic insects; will come to ground feeders offering corn

Compare: The female Blue-winged Teal (pg. 145) is smaller. The female Wood Duck (pg. 155) has a white eye-ring. The female Northern Shoveler (pg. 159) has a spoon-shaped bill.

Stan's Notes: A familiar duck of lakes and ponds, it's considered a type of dabbling duck, tipping forward in shallow water to feed on aquatic plants on the bottom. The name "Mallard" comes from the Latin *masculus*, meaning "male," referring to the habit of males not taking part in raising ducklings. Both female and male have white tails and white underwings. Black central tail feathers of male curl upward. Will return to place of birth.

Ring-necked Pheasant
Phasianus colchicus

Size: 30-36" (76-90 cm), male, including tail
21-25" (53-63 cm), female, including tail

Male: Golden brown body with a long tail. White ring around the neck. A purple, green, blue and red head.

Female: smaller, less flamboyant all-brown bird with a long tail

Juvenile: similar to female, with a shorter tail

Nest: ground; female builds; 1 brood per year

Eggs: 8-10; olive brown without markings

Incubation: 23-25 days; female incubates

Fledging: 11-12 days; female leads young to food

Migration: non-migrator; moves around to find food

Food: insects, seeds, fruit; visits ground feeders

Compare: Male Ring-necked Pheasant is much larger than the female. Both have long tails, but unlike the female Ring-necked, the male is brightly colored.

Stan's Notes: Originally introduced to North America from China in the late 1800s. Common now across the U.S. Like many other game birds, its numbers vary greatly, making it common in some years and scarce in others. Common name "Ring-necked" refers to the thin white ring around the male's neck. "Pheasant" comes from the Greek *phaisianos*, meaning "bird of the River Phasis." (The River Phasis is located in Europe and is now known as the River Rioni.) Listen for the male's cackling call to attract females. Roosts on the ground or in trees at night.

Wild Turkey
Meleagris gallopavo

Size: 36-48" (90-120 cm)

Male: Large, plump brown and bronze bird with a striking blue and red bare head. Fan tail and a long, straight black beard in center of chest. Spurs on legs.

Female: thinner and less striking than male, usually lacking a breast beard

Juvenile: same as adult of the same sex

Nest: ground; female builds; 1 brood per year

Eggs: 10-12; buff white with dull brown markings

Incubation: 27-28 days; female incubates

Fledging: 6-10 days; female leads young to food

Migration: non-migrator; moves around to find food

Food: insects, seeds, fruit

Compare: This bird is quite distinctive and unlikely to be confused with others.

Stan's Notes: The largest native game bird in New York, and the bird from which the domestic turkey was bred. Almost became our national bird, losing to the Bald Eagle by one vote. Eliminated from New York by 1844 due to market hunting and loss of habitat. Was reintroduced during the 1960-1980s. A strong flier; can approach 60 miles (97 km) per hour. Can fly straight up, then away. Eyesight is three times better than human eyesight. Hearing is excellent; able to hear competing males up to a mile away. Males hold "harems" of up to 20 females. Males are called toms, females are hens, young are poults. Roosts in trees at night.

Ruby-crowned Kinglet
Regulus calendula

MIGRATION
SUMMER
WINTER

Size: 4" (10 cm)

Male: Small, teardrop-shaped green-to-gray bird. Two white wing bars and a white eye-ring. Hidden ruby crown.

Female: same as male, but lacking the ruby crown

Juvenile: same as female

Nest: pendulous; female builds; 1 brood per year

Eggs: 4-5; white with brown markings

Incubation: 11-12 days; female incubates

Fledging: 11-12 days; female and male feed young

Migration: complete, to Long Island, southern states, Mexico and Central America

Food: insects, berries

Compare: Golden-crowned Kinglet (pg. 179) lacks a ruby crown. Female American Goldfinch (pg. 273) shares the same color and clear breast, but is larger. Look for the white eye-ring of the Ruby-crowned Kinglet.

Stan's Notes: This is the second smallest bird in New York. Most commonly seen during migration, when groups travel together. Look for it flitting around thick shrubs low to the ground. It takes a quick eye to see the male's ruby crown. Female builds an unusual pendulous (sac-like) nest, intricately woven and decorated on the outside with colored lichens and mosses stuck together with spider webs. Nest is suspended from a branch overlapped by leaves and often hung high in a mature tree. Common name "Kinglet" comes from the Anglo-Saxon word *cyning*, or "king," referring to the male's ruby crown, and the diminutive suffix "let," meaning "small."

Golden-crowned Kinglet
Regulus satrapa

YEAR-ROUND WINTER

Size: 4" (10 cm)

Male: Tiny, plump green-to-gray bird. Distinctive yellow and orange patch with black border on the crown. A white eyebrow mark. Two white wing bars.

Female: same as male, but has a yellow crown with a black border, lacks any orange

Juvenile: same as adults, but lacks gold on crown

Nest: pendulous; female builds; 1-2 broods a year

Eggs: 5-9; white or creamy with brown markings

Incubation: 14-15 days; female incubates

Fledging: 14-19 days; female and male feed young

Migration: complete, to southern states, Mexico and Central America, non-migrator in parts of New York

Food: insects, fruit, tree sap

Compare: Similar to Ruby-crowned Kinglet (pg. 177), but Golden-crowned has an obvious crown. Smaller than the female American Goldfinch (pg. 273), which lacks any crown marking.

Stan's Notes: Often seen in flocks with chickadees, nuthatches, woodpeckers, Brown Creepers and Ruby-crowned Kinglets. While most migrate south, some stay and are commonly seen in winter. Flicks its wings when moving around. Builds an unusual hanging nest, often with moss, lichens and spider webs, and lines it with bark and feathers. Can have so many eggs in its small nest that eggs are in two layers. Drinks tree sap and feeds by gleaning insects from trees. Can be very tame and approachable.

male

female

YEAR-ROUND
WINTER

Red-breasted Nuthatch
Sitta canadensis

Size: 4½" (11 cm)

Male: A small gray-backed bird with a black cap and a prominent eye line. A rust red breast and belly.

Female: gray cap, pale undersides

Juvenile: same as female

Nest: cavity; female builds; 1 brood per year

Eggs: 5-6; white with red brown markings

Incubation: 11-12 days; female incubates

Fledging: 14-20 days; female and male feed young

Migration: irruptive; moves around the state in search of food

Food: insects, seeds; visits seed and suet feeders

Compare: Smaller than the White-breasted Nuthatch (pg. 189), with a red chest instead of white.

Stan's Notes: The Red-breasted Nuthatch behaves like the White-breasted Nuthatch, climbing down tree trunks headfirst. Similar to chickadees, visits seed feeders, quickly grabbing a seed and flying off to crack it open. Will wedge a seed into a crevice and pound it open with several sharp blows. The name "Nuthatch" comes from the Middle English moniker *nuthak*, referring to the bird's habit of wedging a seed into a crevice and hacking it open. Look for it in mature conifers, where it often extracts seeds from cones. Does not excavate a cavity as a chickadee might; rather, it takes over an old woodpecker or chickadee cavity. Common during some winters and scarce in others.

Black-capped Chickadee
Poecile atricapillus

Size: 5" (13 cm)

Male: Familiar gray bird with black cap and throat patch. White chest. Tan belly. Small white wing marks.

Female: same as male

Juvenile: same as adult

Nest: cavity; female and male build or excavate; 1 brood per year

Eggs: 5-7; white with fine brown markings

Incubation: 11-13 days; female and male incubate

Fledging: 14-18 days; female and male feed young

Migration: non-migrator

Food: insects, seeds, fruit; comes to seed and suet feeders

Compare: A familiar backyard bird whose energy and friendliness is hard to mistake.

Stan's Notes: Widespread, common bird throughout New York. Backyard bird that is attracted to a nest box or seed feeder. Usually the first to find a new feeder. Can be easily tamed and hand fed. Can be a common urban bird since much of its diet comes from bird feeders. Needs to feed each day during winter; forages for food even in the worst winter storms. Usually seen with other birds such as nuthatches and woodpeckers. Builds its nest mostly with green moss and lines it with animal fur. The common name comes from its familiar "chika-dee-dee-dee-dee" call. Also gives a high-pitched, two-toned "fee-bee" call. Can have different calls in various regions.

male

first winter

female

Yellow-rumped Warbler
Dendroica coronata

YEAR-ROUND

Size: 5-6" (13-15 cm)

Male: Slate gray bird with black streaks on breast. Yellow patches on rump, flanks and head. White chin and belly. Two white wing bars.

Female: duller than male, but same yellow patches

Juvenile: similar to female

Nest: cup; female builds; 2 broods per year

Eggs: 4-5; white with brown markings

Incubation: 12-13 days; female incubates

Fledging: 10-12 days; female and male feed young

Migration: complete to non-migrator in New York

Food: insects, berries; rarely comes to suet feeders

Compare: The Magnolia Warbler (pg. 277) has more yellow. The male Yellow Warbler (pg. 279) is yellow with orange streaks on the breast. Male Common Yellowthroat (pg. 275) has a yellow breast and distinctive black mask. Palm Warbler (pg. 281) has a yellow throat and chestnut cap.

Stan's Notes: One of our most common warblers and also one of the few warblers to spend the winter in the state. Migrators in flocks of hundreds usually arrive in late September to early October. Male molts to a dull color in winter similar to the female and retains the yellow patches. Often called Myrtle Warbler in eastern states and Audubon's Warbler in western states. Sometimes called Butter-butts due to the yellow patch on its rump. Familiar call is a single robust "chip," heard mostly during migration. Also has a wonderful song in spring.

female
pg. 91

male

Dark-eyed Junco
Junco hyemalis

YEAR-ROUND
WINTER

Size: 5½" (14 cm)

Male: Round, dark-eyed bird with a slate gray-to-charcoal chest, head and back. White belly. Pink bill. Since the outermost tail feathers are white, tail appears as a white V in flight.

Female: same as male, only tan-to-brown color

Juvenile: similar to female, but has a streaked breast and head

Nest: cup; female and male construct; 2 broods per year

Eggs: 3-5; white with reddish brown markings

Incubation: 12-13 days; female incubates

Fledging: 10-13 days; male and female feed young

Migration: complete, across the U.S., non-migrator in parts of New York

Food: seeds, insects; will come to seed feeders

Compare: Rarely confused with any other bird. Small flocks feed under bird feeders in winter.

Stan's Notes: One of the most common winter birds in New York. Migrates from Canada to New York and beyond. Small population stays in the state year-round. Females tend to migrate farther south than the males. Adheres to a rigid social hierarchy, with dominant birds chasing the less dominant birds. Look for its white outer tail feathers flashing when in flight. Usually seen in small flocks on the ground, where it "double-scratches" with both feet simultaneously to expose seeds and insects. Eats many weed seeds. Nests in a wide variety of wooded habitats. Several junco species have now been combined into one, simply called Dark-eyed Junco.

White-breasted Nuthatch

Sitta carolinensis

YEAR-ROUND

Size: 5-6" (13-15 cm)

Male: Slate gray with a white face and belly, and black cap and nape. Long thin bill, slightly upturned. Chestnut undertail.

Female: similar to male, gray cap and nape

Juvenile: similar to female

Nest: cavity; female and male construct; 1 brood per year

Eggs: 5-7; white with brown markings

Incubation: 11-12 days; female incubates

Fledging: 13-14 days; female and male feed young

Migration: non-migrator

Food: insects, seeds; visits seed and suet feeders

Compare: Red-breasted Nuthatch (pg. 181) is smaller with a rust red belly and a distinctive black eye line.

Stan's Notes: The nuthatch's habit of hopping headfirst down tree trunks helps it see insects and insect eggs that birds climbing up the trunk might miss. Incredible climbing agility comes from an extra-long hind toe claw or nail, nearly twice the size of the front toe claws. The name "Nuthatch" comes from the Middle English moniker *nuthak*, referring to the bird's habit of wedging a seed into a crevice and hacking it open. Often seen in flocks with chickadees, Brown Creepers and Downy Woodpeckers. Mated birds will stay with each other year-round, defending small territories. Listen for its characteristic spring call, "whi-whi-whi-whi," given in February and March. One of 17 worldwide nuthatch species.

Tufted Titmouse
Baeolophus bicolor

Size: 6" (15 cm)

Male: Slate gray bird with a white chest and belly. Pointed crest. Flanks are washed with rusty brown. Gray legs and dark eyes.

Female: same as male

Juvenile: same as adult

Nest: cavity; female lines old woodpecker hole; 2 broods per year

Eggs: 5-7; white with brown markings

Incubation: 13-14 days; female incubates

Fledging: 15-18 days; female and male feed young

Migration: non-migrator

Food: insects, seeds, fruit; will come to seed and suet feeders

Compare: Closely related to the slightly smaller Black-capped Chickadee (pg. 183), but the Tufted Titmouse has a crest. Similar size and color as the White-breasted Nuthatch (pg. 189), but the Nuthatch lacks a crest.

Stan's Notes: A common feeder bird, it can be attracted with black oil sunflower seeds. Well known for its quickly repeated "peter-peter-peter" call. The prefix "Tit" comes from a Scandinavian word meaning "little." Suffix "mouse" is derived from the Old English word *mase*, meaning "bird." Simply translated, it is a "small bird." Notorious for pulling hair from sleeping dogs, cats and squirrels to line their nests. Attracted with nest boxes. Usually seen only one or two at a time. Male feeds female during courtship and nesting.

Eastern Phoebe
Sayornis phoebe

Size: 7" (18 cm)

Male: Gray bird with dark wings, light olive green belly and a thin dark bill.

Female: same as male

Juvenile: same as adult

Nest: cup; female builds; 2 broods per year

Eggs: 4-5; white without markings

Incubation: 15-16 days; female incubates

Fledging: 15-16 days; male and female feed young

Migration: complete, to southern states and Mexico

Food: insects

Compare: Like most other olive gray birds, it is hard to distinguish identifying markings. Eastern Phoebe lacks any white eye-ring. Easier to identify by well-enunciated song, "fee-bee," or characteristic of hawking for insects.

Stan's Notes: A sparrow-sized bird often seen on the end of a dead branch. It sits in wait for a passing insect, flies out to catch it, then returns to the same branch, a process called hawking. Has a habit of pumping its tail up and down and spreading it when perched. Will build its nest under the eaves of a house, under a bridge or in culverts. Nest is constructed with mud, grass and moss, and lined with hair (and sometimes feathers). The name is derived from its characteristic song, "fee-bee," which is repeated over and over from the tops of dead branches.

Great Crested Flycatcher
Myiarchus crinitus

Size: 8" (20 cm)

Male: Gray head with prominent crest. Gray back and throat with bright yellow belly, yellow extending under reddish brown tail. Lower bill is yellow at base.

Female: same as male

Juvenile: same as adult

Nest: cavity; female and male construct; 1 brood per year

Eggs: 4-6; white or buff with brown markings

Incubation: 13-15 days; female incubates

Fledging: 14-21 days; female and male feed young

Migration: complete, to Mexico and Central America

Food: insects, fruit

Compare: The Eastern Kingbird (pg. 201) has a white band across the tail. Similar to the Eastern Phoebe (pg. 193), but the Great Crested Flycatcher has a crest and yellow belly.

Stan's Notes: Common bird of wooded areas in New York. Breeds throughout most of the state. Lives high up in trees, rarely coming to the ground. Often heard before seen. The first part of its common name refers to the set of extra long feathers on top of head (crest), which the bird raises when alert or agitated, similar to the Northern Cardinal. Feeds by gleaning insects from tree leaves. Nests in old woodpecker cavities, but can be attracted to a nest box with a 1½-2½-inch (4-6 cm) entrance hole placed high in a tree. Usually stuffs its nest with a collection of fur, feathers, string and snakeskins.

breeding
pg. 119

winter

Sanderling
Calidris alba

MIGRATION
WINTER

Size: 8" (20 cm)

Male: The lightest sandpiper on the beach during winter. Winter plumage head and back are gray and belly is white. Black legs and bill. White wing stripe, seen only in flight.

Female: same as male

Juvenile: spotty black on the head and back, a white belly, black legs and bill

Nest: ground; male builds; 1-2 broods per year

Eggs: 3-4; greenish olive with brown markings

Incubation: 24-30 days; male and female incubate

Fledging: 16-17 days; female and male feed young

Migration: complete, to the East and Gulf coasts, West Indies, Mexico, Central and South America

Food: insects

Compare: Same size as Spotted Sandpiper (pg. 117) and similar to the winter plumage Spotted. The winter Black-bellied Plover (pg. 213) is much larger with a larger bill.

Stan's Notes: Very common shorebird in New York. Can be seen in groups on sandy beaches, running out with each retreating wave to feed. Look for flash of white on wings when it is in flight. Sometimes a female will mate with several males (polyandry), which results in males and the female incubating separate nests. Both sexes perform distraction displays if threatened. Stands on one leg to rest and tucks the other into its belly feathers. Often hops on one leg, moving away from pedestrians on beaches. Surveys show population declines of greater than 80 percent since the 1970s. Nests on the Arctic tundra.

winter

breeding
pg. 121

Dunlin
Calidris alpina

MIGRATION
WINTER

Size: 8-9" (20-22.5 cm)

Male: Winter adult has a brownish gray back with a light gray chest and white belly. Stout bill curves slightly downward at tip. Black legs.

Female: slightly larger than male, with a longer bill

Juvenile: slightly rusty back with a spotty chest

Nest: ground; male and female construct; 1 brood per year

Eggs: 2-4; olive buff or blue green with red brown markings

Incubation: 21-22 days; male and female incubate, male incubates during the day, female at night

Fledging: 19-21 days; male feeds young, female often leaves before young fledge

Migration: complete, to Long Island, the East and Gulf coasts, Mexico and Central America

Food: insects

Compare: Similar size as winter Sanderling (pg. 197), but the winter Dunlin has a longer down-turned bill and is an overall darker gray.

Stan's Notes: Flights include heights of up to 100 feet (30 m) with brief gliding alternating with shallow flutters, and a rhythmic, repeating song. Huge flocks fly synchronously, with birds twisting and turning, flashing light and dark undersides. Males tend to fly farther south in winter than females. Winter visitor in Long Island. Doesn't nest in New York.

Eastern Kingbird
Tyrannus tyrannus

SUMMER

Size: 8½" (22 cm)

Male: Mostly black gray bird with white belly and chin. Black head and tail with a distinctive white band across the end of the tail. Has a concealed red crown that is rarely seen.

Female: same as male

Juvenile: same as adult

Nest: cup; male and female construct; 1 brood per year

Eggs: 3-4; white with brown markings

Incubation: 16-18 days; female incubates

Fledging: 16-18 days; female and male feed young

Migration: complete, to Mexico, Central America and South America

Food: insects, fruit

Compare: Medium-sized bird, smaller than American Robin (pg. 209). Eastern Phoebe (pg. 193) is smaller and lacks Kingbird's white belly. Look for a white band on the Kingbird's tail.

Stan's Notes: A summer resident seen in open fields and prairies. Up to 20 individuals migrate together in a group. Returns to the mating ground in springtime, where male and female defend their territory. Acting unafraid of other birds and chasing the larger ones, it is perceived as having an attitude. Its bold behavior gave rise to the common name, King. Perches on tall branches and watches for insects. After flying out to catch them, returns to the same perch, a technique called hawking. Becomes very vocal during late summer, when entire families call back and forth while hunting for insects.

male pg. 257

female

Pine Grosbeak
Pinicola enucleator

Size: 9" (22.5 cm)

Female: A plump gray winter finch with a long dark tail. Dark wings. Two white wing bars. Head and rump tinged dull yellow. Short, stubby, pointed dark bill.

Male: overall rosy red and gray

Juvenile: female is similar to adult female, male has a touch of red on head and rump

Nest: cup; female builds; 1 brood per year

Eggs: 4-5; bluish green without markings

Incubation: 13-15 days; female incubates

Fledging: 13-20 days; female and male feed young

Migration: irruptive; moves around to find food

Food: seeds, fruit, insects; will come to feeders

Compare: The female Evening Grosbeak (pg. 291) is slightly smaller and lacks the dull yellow head of the female Pine Grosbeak.

Stan's Notes: This winter finch is common in New York in some years and not so common in others. A very tame and approachable bird. Often seen along roads or on the ground, eating tiny grains of sand and dirt to aid digestion. A seed eater that favors coniferous forests, rarely moving out of coniferous regions during summer. Frequently seen bathing in fluffy snow. Flies with a typical finch-like undulating pattern while it calls a soft whistle. During breeding season, the male and female develop a pouch in the bottom of the mouth (buccal pouch) to transport seeds to young.

Gray Catbird
Dumetella carolinensis

YEAR-ROUND
SUMMER

Size: 9" (22.5 cm)

Male: Handsome slate gray bird with black crown and a long, thin black bill. Often seen with its tail lifted up, exposing a chestnut patch under the tail.

Female: same as male

Juvenile: same as adult

Nest: cup; female and male construct; 2 broods per year

Eggs: 4-6; blue green without markings

Incubation: 12-13 days; female incubates

Fledging: 10-11 days; female and male feed young

Migration: complete, to southern states

Food: insects, fruit

Compare: Larger than Eastern Phoebe (pg. 193), it lacks the Phoebe's olive belly. Similar size as Eastern Kingbird (pg. 201), but it lacks the Kingbird's white belly and white tail band.

Stan's Notes: A secretive bird that the Chippewa Indians named Bird That Cries With Grief due to its raspy call. The call sounds like the mewing of a house cat, hence the common name. Frequently mimics other birds, rarely repeating the same phrases. More often heard than seen. Nests in thick shrubs and quickly flies back into shrubs if approached. If a cowbird introduces an egg into a catbird nest, the catbird will quickly break it, then eject it.

red morph

gray morph

Eastern Screech-Owl

Megascops asio

YEAR-ROUND

Size: 9" (22.5 cm); up to 20-inch wingspan

Male: Small "eared" owl that occurs in one of two permanent color morphs. Is either mottled with gray and white or is red brown (rust) with white. Bright yellow eyes.

Female: same as male

Juvenile: lighter color than adult of the same morph, usually no ear tufts

Nest: cavity, former woodpecker cavity; does not add any nesting material; 1 brood per year

Eggs: 4-5; white without markings

Incubation: 25-26 days; female incubates, male feeds female during incubation

Fledging: 26-27 days; male and female feed young

Migration: non-migrator

Food: large insects, small mammals, birds, snakes

Compare: This is the only small owl in New York with ear tufts. Can be gray or rust in color.

Stan's Notes: A common owl active at dusk and during the night. Excellent hearing and eyesight. Will seldom give a screeching call; more commonly gives a tremulous, descending whiny trill, like a sound effect of a scary movie. Will nest in a wooden nest box. Often seen sunning themselves at nest box holes during the winter. Male and female may roost together at night, and are thought to mate for life. Different colorations are known as morphs. The gray morph is more common than the red.

male

female

American Robin
Turdus migratorius

YEAR-ROUND
SUMMER

Size: 9-11" (22.5-28 cm)

Male: A familiar gray bird with a rusty red breast and nearly black head and tail. White chin with black streaks. White eye-ring.

Female: similar to male, but with a gray head and a duller breast

Juvenile: similar to female, but has a speckled breast and brown back

Nest: cup; female builds with help from the male; 2-3 broods per year

Eggs: 4-7; pale blue without markings

Incubation: 12-14 days; female incubates

Fledging: 14-16 days; female and male feed young

Migration: complete to non-migrator in New York

Food: insects, fruit, berries, earthworms

Compare: Familiar bird to all.

Stan's Notes: Can be heard singing all night long during spring. Most people don't realize how easy it is to differentiate between male and female robins. Compare the male's dark, nearly black head and brick red breast with the female's gray head and dull red breast. Robins are not listening for worms when they cock their heads to one side. They are looking with eyes placed far back on the sides of their heads. A very territorial bird. Frequently seen fighting its own reflection in windows. Although robins are complete migrators in northern states, a small percentage in New York are non-migrators. Non-migrators spend the winter in low swampy areas, where they search for leftover berries and insect eggs.

displaying

Northern Mockingbird
Mimus polyglottos

YEAR-ROUND

Size: 10" (25 cm)

Male: Silvery gray head and back with light gray chest and belly. White wing patches, seen in flight or during display. Tail mostly black with white outer tail feathers. Black bill.

Female: same as male

Juvenile: dull gray, a heavily streaked chest, gray bill

Nest: cup; female and male build; 2 broods per year, sometimes more

Eggs: 3-5; blue green with brown markings

Incubation: 12-13 days; female incubates

Fledging: 11-13 days; female and male feed young

Migration: non-migrator to partial in New York; will move around to find food

Food: insects, fruit

Compare: The Gray Catbird (pg. 205) is slate gray and lacks wing patches. Look for Mockingbird to spread its wings, flash its white wing patches and wag its tail from side to side.

Stan's Notes: Very animated bird. Performs an elaborate mating dance. Facing each other with heads and tails erect, pairs will run toward each other, flashing white wing patches, and then retreat to cover nearby. Thought to flash wing patches to scare up bugs when hunting. Sits for long periods on top of a shrub. Imitates other birds (vocal mimicry), hence the common name. Young males often sing at night. Often unafraid of people, allowing for close observation.

breeding
pg. 37

winter

Black-bellied Plover
Pluvialis squatarola

MIGRATION SUMMER

Size: 11-12" (28-30 cm)

Male: Winter plumage is uniform light gray with dark, nearly black streaks. White belly and chest. Faint white eyebrow mark. Black legs and bill.

Female: less black on belly and breast than male

Juvenile: grayer than adults, with much less black

Nest: ground; male and female construct; 1 brood per year

Eggs: 3-4; pinkish or greenish with black brown markings

Incubation: 26-27 days; male and female incubate, male incubates during the day, female at night

Fledging: 35-45 days; male feeds young, young learn quickly to feed themselves

Migration: complete, to the East and Gulf coasts, West Indies, Mexico, Central and South America

Food: insects

Compare: Winter Dunlin (pg. 199) has a long down-curved bill. Winter Sanderling (pg. 197) has a smaller bill. Winter Spotted Sandpiper (pg. 117) has a shorter, thicker bill.

Stan's Notes: Male performs a "butterfly" courtship flight to attract females. Female leaves the male and young about 12 days after the eggs hatch. Starts breeding at 3 years of age. Begins fall migration in July and August. During flight, in any plumage, displays a white rump and stripe on wings with black axillaries (armpits). Will often dart across the ground to grab an insect and run.

CD 1, TRACK 18

YEAR-ROUND

Gray Jay
Perisoreus canadensis

Size: 11½" (29 cm)

Male: A large gray bird with black nape and white chest. Short black bill and dark eyes. White patch on forehead.

Female: same as male

Juvenile: sooty gray with a faint white whisker mark

Nest: cup; male and female construct; 1 brood per year

Eggs: 3-4; gray white, finely marked to unmarked

Incubation: 16-18 days; female incubates

Fledging: 14-15 days; male and female feed young

Migration: non-migrator

Food: insects, seeds, fruit, nuts; visits seed feeder

Compare: Similar size as Blue Jay (pg. 67), but lacks the Blue Jay's crest and blue coloring.

Stan's Notes: A bird of northern woods. Known as Camp Robber because it rummages through camps looking for food scraps. Also called Whisky Jack or Canada Jay. Easily tamed, this bird will fly to your hand if offered raisins or nuts. Will eat just about anything. Also stores extra food for the winter, balling it together in a sticky mass, placing it on a tree branch, often concealing it with lichen or bark. Travels around in small family units of 3-5, making good companions for campers and canoeists. Reminds some people of an overgrown chickadee.

YEAR-ROUND

Rock Pigeon
Columba livia

Size: 13" (33 cm)

Male: No set color pattern. Gray to white, patches of iridescent greens and blues, usually with a light rump patch.

Female: same as male

Juvenile: same as adult

Nest: platform; female builds; 3-4 broods per year

Eggs: 1-2; white without markings

Incubation: 18-20 days; female and male incubate

Fledging: 25-26 days; female and male feed young

Migration: non-migrator

Food: seeds

Compare: Mourning Dove (pg. 139) is smaller, light brown and lacks all the color variations of the Rock Pigeon.

Stan's Notes: Also known as Domestic Pigeon, formerly known as Rock Dove. Introduced to North America from Europe by the early settlers. This bird is most common around cities and barnyards, where it scratches for seeds. One of the few birds that has a wide variety of colors, produced by years of selective breeding while in captivity. Parents feed their young a regurgitated liquid known as crop-milk for the first few days of life. One of the few birds that can drink without tilting its head back. Nests under bridges and on buildings, balconies, barns and sheds. Was once poisoned as a "nuisance city bird." Many cities now have Peregrine Falcons (not shown) that feed on Rock Pigeons, keeping their numbers in check.

CD 2, TRACK 39

soaring

juvenile

Sharp-shinned Hawk
Accipiter striatus

YEAR-ROUND

Size: 10-14" (25-36 cm); up to 2-foot wingspan

Male: Small woodland hawk with a gray back and head and a rusty red breast. Long tail with several dark tail bands, widest band at end of squared-off tail. Red eyes.

Female: same as male, only larger

Juvenile: same size as adults, with a brown back and heavily streaked breast, yellow eyes

Nest: platform; female builds; 1 brood per year

Eggs: 4-5; white with brown markings

Incubation: 32-35 days; female incubates

Fledging: 24-27 days; female and male feed young

Migration: non-migrator to partial in New York

Food: birds, small mammals

Compare: Very similar to Cooper's Hawk (pg. 221), only smaller. The Cooper's has a larger head, slightly longer neck and rounded tail. Look for the Sharp-shinned Hawk's squared tail to help identify.

Stan's Notes: A common hawk of backyards and woodlands, often seen swooping in on birds visiting feeders. Its short rounded wings and long tail allow this hawk to navigate through thick stands of trees in pursuit of prey. Common name comes from the sharp keel on the leading edge of its "shin," though it is actually below rather than above the bird's ankle on the tarsus bone of foot. The tarsus in most birds is round. In flight, head doesn't protrude as far as the head of the Cooper's Hawk.

soaring

juvenile

Cooper's Hawk
Accipiter cooperii

YEAR-ROUND

Size: 14-20" (36-50 cm); up to 2½-foot wingspan

Male: Medium-sized hawk with short wings and long rounded tail with several black bands. Rusty breast and dark wing tips. Slate gray back. Bright yellow spot at base of gray bill (cere). Dark red eyes.

Female: similar to male, only slightly larger

Juvenile: brown back with brown streaks on breast, bright yellow eyes

Nest: platform; male and female build; 1 brood per year

Eggs: 2-4; greenish with brown markings

Incubation: 32-36 days; female and male incubate

Fledging: 28-32 days; male and female feed young

Migration: non-migrator to partial in New York; will move around to find food

Food: small birds, mammals

Compare: Nearly identical to the Sharp-shinned Hawk (pg. 219), only larger, darker gray and with a rounded-off tail.

Stan's Notes: A common year-round resident hawk of woodlands. During flight, look for its large head, short wings and long tail. The stubby wings help it maneuver between trees while pursuing small birds. Comes to feeders, hunting for unaware birds. Flies with long glides followed by a few quick flaps. Known to ambush prey, it will fly into heavy brush or even run on the ground in pursuit. Nestlings have gray eyes that become bright yellow at 1 year and dark red later.

female
pg. 169

male

soaring

Northern Harrier
Circus cyaneus

YEAR-ROUND SUMMER

Size: 22½" (57 cm); up to 3½-foot wingspan

Male: A slim, low-flying hawk. Silver gray with a large white rump patch and a white belly. Faint narrow bands across tail. Black wing tips. Yellow eyes.

Female: dark brown back, a brown-streaked breast and belly, large white rump patch, narrow black bands across the tail, black wing tips, yellow eyes

Juvenile: similar to female, with an orange breast

Nest: platform, often on ground; female and male build; 1 brood per year

Eggs: 4-8; bluish white without markings

Incubation: 31-32 days; female incubates

Fledging: 30-35 days; male and female feed young

Migration: partial to non-migrator in New York

Food: mice, snakes, insects, small birds

Compare: Slimmer than Red-tailed Hawk (pg. 165). Look for black tail bands, white rump patch and characteristic flight to help identify.

Stan's Notes: One of the easiest hawks to identify. Harriers glide just above ground, following contours of the land while searching for prey. Holds its wings just above the horizontal position, tilting back and forth in the wind, similar to Turkey Vultures. Formerly called Marsh Hawk due to its habit of hunting over marshes. Feeds on the ground. Will perch on the ground to preen and rest. At any age, has a distinctive owl-like face disk.

in flight

YEAR-ROUND

Canada Goose
Branta canadensis

Size: 25-43" (63-109 cm); up to 5½-foot wingspan

Male: Large gray goose with a black neck and head and a white chin or cheek strap.

Female: same as male

Juvenile: same as adult

Nest: platform, on the ground; female builds; 1 brood per year

Eggs: 5-10; white without markings

Incubation: 25-30 days; female incubates

Fledging: 42-55 days; male and female teach young to feed

Migration: non-migrator

Food: aquatic plants, insects, seeds

Compare: Large goose that is rarely confused with any other bird.

Stan's Notes: This bird is a year-round resident in the state. Adults will mate for many years, but only start to breed in their third year. Males often act as sentinels, standing at the edge of their group and bobbing their heads up and down, becoming very aggressive to anybody who approaches. Will hiss as if displaying displeasure. Adults molt primary flight feathers while raising young, rendering family groups flightless at the same time. Several subspecies vary geographically across the U.S. Generally they are paler in color in eastern groups and darker in western. Size decreases northward, with the smallest subspecies found on the Arctic tundra.

in flight

Great Blue Heron
Ardea herodias

YEAR-ROUND
SUMMER

Size: 42-52" (107-132 cm); up to 6-foot wingspan

Male: Tall gray heron. Black eyebrows extend into several long plumes off the back of head. Long yellow bill. Feathers at base of neck drop down in a kind of necklace.

Female: same as male

Juvenile: same as adult, but more brown than gray, with a black crown and no plumes

Nest: platform; male and female build; 1 brood per year

Eggs: 3-5; blue green without markings

Incubation: 27-28 days; female and male incubate

Fledging: 56-60 days; male and female feed young

Migration: complete, to southern states, Mexico and Central and South America, non-migrator in parts of New York

Food: small fish, frogs, insects, snakes

Compare: Larger in size and similar in shape to the Great Egret (pg. 267), which is all white.

Stan's Notes: One of the most common herons, often barking like a dog when startled. Seen stalking small fish in shallow water. Strikes at mice, squirrels and just about anything else it might come across. Flies holding neck in an S shape, with its long legs trailing straight out behind. Wings are held in cupped fashion during flight. Nests in treetops near or over open water in colonies of up to 100 birds.

CD 2, TRACK 43

male

female

Ruby-throated Hummingbird
Archilochus colubris

Size: 3-3½" (7.5-9 cm)

Male: Tiny iridescent green bird with black throat patch that reflects bright ruby red in sun.

Female: same as male, but lacking the throat patch

Juvenile: same as female

Nest: cup; female builds; 1-2 broods per year

Eggs: 2; white without markings

Incubation: 12-14 days; female incubates

Fledging: 14-18 days; female feeds young

Migration: complete, to southern states, Mexico and Central America

Food: nectar, insects; will come to nectar feeders

Compare: No other bird is as tiny. The Sphinx Moth also hovers at flowers, but has clear wings and a mouth part that looks like a straw, which coils up when not at flowers. Doesn't hum in flight, moves much slower than the Hummingbird and can be approached.

Stan's Notes: The smallest bird in New York. Can hover, fly up and down, and is the only bird to fly backward. Does not sing, but will chatter or buzz to communicate. The wings create a humming noise, flapping 50-60 times each second or faster during chasing flights. The heart pumps an incredible 1,260 beats per minute, and it breathes 250 times per minute. Weighing just 2-3 grams, it takes about five average-sized hummingbirds to equal the weight of one chickadee. Constructs its nest with plant material and spider webs, gluing pieces of lichen on the outside for camouflage. Attracted to tubular red flowers.

female pg. 155

male

Wood Duck
Aix sponsa

SUMMER

Size: 17-20" (43-50 cm)

Male: A small, highly ornamented dabbling duck with a green head and crest patterned with white and black. A rusty chest, white belly and red eyes.

Female: brown, similar size and shape as male, has bright white eye-ring and a not-so-obvious crest, blue patch on wing often hidden

Juvenile: same as female

Nest: cavity; female lines old woodpecker cavity; 1 brood per year

Eggs: 10-15; creamy white without markings

Incubation: 28-36 days; female incubates

Fledging: 56-68 days; female teaches young to feed

Migration: complete, to southern states

Food: aquatic insects, plants, seeds

Compare: The male Northern Shoveler (pg. 235) has a long wide bill. Male Hooded Merganser (pg. 41) is similar in size, but has a "hood."

Stan's Notes: A common duck of quiet, shallow backwater ponds. Nearly extinct around 1900 due to overhunting, but is doing well now. Nests in an old woodpecker hole or uses a nesting box. Often seen flying deep in forests or perched high on tree branches. Female takes to flight with a loud squealing call and enters nest cavity from full flight. Lays eggs in a neighboring female nest (egg dumping), resulting in some clutches in excess of 20 eggs. Young stay in nest 24 hours after hatching, then jump from up to 30 feet (9 m) to the ground or water to follow their mother, never returning to the nest.

Green Heron
Butorides virescens

SUMMER

Size: 16-22" (40-56 cm)

Male: Short stocky heron with a blue-green back, and rusty red neck and breast. Dark green crest. Short legs, normally yellow, but turn bright orange during breeding season.

Female: same as male

Juvenile: similar to adult, with a blue-gray back and white-streaked breast and neck

Nest: platform; female and male build; 2 broods per year

Eggs: 2-4; light green without markings

Incubation: 21-25 days; female and male incubate

Fledging: 35-36 days; female and male feed young

Migration: complete, to South America

Food: fish, insects, amphibians, aquatic plants

Compare: Much smaller than the Great Blue Heron (pg. 227) and lacks the long neck of most other herons. Look for a small heron with a dark green back stalking wetlands.

Stan's Notes: Often gives an explosive, rasping "skyew" call when startled. Sometimes it looks like it doesn't have a neck, because it holds its head close to its body. Hunts for small fish, aquatic insects and small amphibians by waiting on a shore or wading stealthily. Known to place an object such as an insect on the water surface to attract fish to catch. Raises its crest when excited.

female pg. 159

male

Northern Shoveler
Anas clypeata

Size: 20" (50 cm)

Male: Medium-sized duck with iridescent green head, rusty sides and white breast. Has an extraordinarily large spoon-shaped bill that is almost always held pointed toward water.

Female: brown and black all over, green speculum, spoon-shaped bill

Juvenile: same as female

Nest: ground; female builds; 1 brood per year

Eggs: 9-12; olive without markings

Incubation: 22-25 days; female incubates

Fledging: 30-60 days; female leads young to food

Migration: complete, to New York, southern states, Mexico and Central America

Food: aquatic insects, plants

Compare: Similar to the male Mallard (pg. 239), but Shoveler has a large, characteristic spoon-shaped bill. Larger than male Wood Duck (pg. 231) and lacks the Wood Duck's crest.

Stan's Notes: One of several species of shoveler, so called because of the peculiar shape of its bill. The Northern Shoveler is the only species of these ducks in North America. Found in small flocks of 5-10, swimming low in water with its large bill pointed toward the water, as if it's too heavy to lift. Feeds mainly by filtering tiny aquatic insects and plants from the water's surface with its bill.

in flight

female pg. 259

male

Common Merganser
Mergus merganser

MIGRATION
SUMMER
WINTER

Size: 25" (63 cm)

Male: Long, thin, duck-like bird with green head, black back and white sides, chest and neck. Long, pointed orange bill. Often appears to be black and white in poor light.

Female: same size and shape as the male, but with a rust red head, ragged "hair" on head, gray body with white chest and chin, and long, pointed orange bill

Juvenile: same as female

Nest: cavity; female lines old woodpecker cavity; 1 brood per year

Eggs: 9-11; ivory without markings

Incubation: 28-33 days; female incubates

Fledging: 70-80 days; female feeds young

Migration: complete, to New York, southern states, Mexico and Central America

Food: small fish, aquatic insects

Compare: Male Mallard (pg. 239) has a green head, but lacks the black back, bright white sides and long pointed bill.

Stan's Notes: The merganser is a shallow water diver that feeds on small fish in 10-15 feet (3-4.5 m) of water. Bill has a fine serrated-like edge to help catch slippery fish. Females often lay eggs in other merganser nests (egg dumping), resulting in broods of up to 15 young per mother. Male leaves female when she starts to incubate her eggs. Orphans are accepted by other merganser mothers with young. Can be seen on just about any open water during winter.

female pg. 171

male

YEAR-ROUND

Mallard
Anas platyrhynchos

Size: 25" (63 cm)

Male: Large, bulbous green head, white necklace and rust brown or chestnut chest. Gray and white on the sides. Yellow bill. Orange legs and feet.

Female: brown duck with an orange and black bill and blue and white wing mark (speculum)

Juvenile: same as female, but with a yellow bill

Nest: ground; female builds; 1 brood per year

Eggs: 7-10; greenish to whitish, unmarked

Incubation: 26-30 days; female incubates

Fledging: 42-52 days; female leads young to food

Migration: non-migrator to partial in New York

Food: seeds, plants, aquatic insects; will come to ground feeders offering corn

Compare: Most people recognize this common duck. Male Shoveler (pg. 235) has a white chest with rust on sides and a spoon-shaped bill.

Stan's Notes: A familiar duck of lakes and ponds, it's considered a type of dabbling duck, tipping forward in shallow water to feed on aquatic plants on the bottom. The name "Mallard" comes from the Latin *masculus*, meaning "male," referring to the habit of males not taking part in raising ducklings. Black central tail feathers of male curl upward. Both the male and female have white tails and white underwings. Will return to place of birth.

female pg. 271

male

SUMMER

American Redstart
Setophaga ruticilla

Size: 5" (13 cm)

Male: Small, striking black bird with contrasting patches of orange on sides, wings and tail. White belly.

Female: olive brown with yellow patches on sides, wings and tail, white belly

Juvenile: same as female, the juvenile male is tinged orange in the first year

Nest: cup; female builds; 1 brood per year

Eggs: 3-5; off-white with brown markings

Incubation: 12 days; female incubates

Fledging: 9 days; female and male feed young

Migration: complete, to Mexico, Central America and South America

Food: insects, seeds, berries rarely

Compare: Male Red-winged Blackbird (pg. 9) and the male Baltimore Oriole (pg. 243) are much larger at roughly 8 inches (20 cm). The only small black and orange bird flitting around the tops of trees.

Stan's Notes: This is a common and widespread breeding warbler in New York. Prefers large unbroken tracts of forest. Appears to be hyperactive when feeding, hovering and darting back and forth to glean insects from leaves. Often droops its wings and fans tail just before launching out to catch an insect. Look for the male's flashing black and orange colors high up in trees.

male

female pg. 287

Baltimore Oriole
Icterus galbula

SUMMER

Size: 7-8" (18-20 cm)

Male: Bright flaming orange bird with black head and black extending down nape of neck onto the back. Black wings with white and orange wing bars. An orange tail with black streaks. Gray bill and dark eyes.

Female: pale yellow with orange tones, gray brown wings, white wing bars, gray bill, dark eyes

Juvenile: same as female

Nest: pendulous; female builds; 1 brood per year

Eggs: 4-5; bluish with brown markings

Incubation: 12-14 days; female incubates

Fledging: 12-14 days; female and male feed young

Migration: complete, to Mexico, Central America and South America

Food: insects, fruit, nectar; comes to orange half and nectar feeders

Compare: Male Orchard Oriole (pg. 245) is a much darker orange than the flaming orange of the Baltimore. The male Redstart (pg. 241) is smaller and has more black than orange.

Stan's Notes: A fantastic songster, this bird usually is heard before seen. Easily attracted to a feeder offering grape jelly, orange halves or sugar water (nectar). Parents bring young to feeders. Sits in tops of trees feeding on caterpillars. Female builds a sock-like nest at the outermost branches of tall trees. Often returns to the same area year after year. Some of the last birds to arrive in spring (May) and first to leave in fall (September).

CD 2, TRACK 48

female
pg. 289

male

Orchard Oriole
Icterus spurius

Size: 7-8" (18-20 cm)

Male: Dull orange oriole with a black head, chin, wings and tail, and black extending down the back. Single white wing bars. Long, thin black bill with a small gray mark on lower mandible (jaw).

Female: olive green back with a dull yellow belly, 2 white wing bars on dark gray wings

Juvenile: same as female, black bib on first-year male

Nest: pendulous; female builds; 1 brood per year

Eggs: 3-5; pale blue to white, brown markings

Incubation: 11-12 days; female and male incubate

Fledging: 11-14 days; female and male feed young

Migration: complete, to Mexico, Central America and northern South America

Food: insects, fruit; comes to fruit/nectar feeders

Compare: Similar to male Baltimore Oriole (pg. 243), but the male Orchard Oriole has a much darker orange body.

Stan's Notes: Prefers orchards or open woods, hence its common name. Eats insects until wild fruit starts to ripen. One of the last birds to arrive in spring and one of the first to leave in fall. Spends 3-4 months in New York. Often migrates with the more abundant Baltimore Oriole. Frequently nests alone, but sometimes nests in small colonies. Parents bring young to jelly and orange half feeders just after fledging. Many people think the orioles have left during summer, but the birds are concentrating on finding insects to feed their young. Common in the southern half of New York.

male

female pg. 81

yellow male

YEAR-ROUND

House Finch
Carpodacus mexicanus

Size: 5" (13 cm)

Male: An orange red face, breast and rump, with a brown cap. Brown marking behind eyes. Brown wings streaked with white. A white belly with brown streaks.

Female: brown with a heavily streaked white chest

Juvenile: similar to female

Nest: cup, sometimes in cavities; female builds; 2 broods per year

Eggs: 4-5; pale blue, lightly marked

Incubation: 12-14 days; female incubates

Fledging: 15-19 days; female and male feed young

Migration: non-migrator to partial; will move around to find food

Food: seeds, fruit, leaf buds; will visit seed feeders

Compare: Male Purple Finch (pg. 249) is very similar, but male House Finch lacks the red crown. Look for the streaked breast and belly, and brown cap of male House Finch.

Stan's Notes: Very social bird. Visits feeders in small flocks. Likes nesting in hanging flower baskets. Incubating female is fed by the male. Has a loud, cheerful warbling song. House Finches that were originally introduced to Long Island, New York, from the western U.S. in the 1940s have since populated the entire eastern U.S. Now found throughout the country. Can be the most common bird at your feeders. Suffers from a fatal eye disease that causes the eyes to crust over. Rarely, some males are yellow (see inset) instead of red, probably due to poor diet.

female
pg. 95

male

Purple Finch
Carpodacus purpureus

YEAR-ROUND
WINTER

Size: 6" (15 cm)

Male: Raspberry red head, cap, breast, back and rump. Brownish wings and tail.

Female: heavily streaked brown and white bird with large white eyebrows

Juvenile: same as female

Nest: cup; female and male construct; 1 brood per year

Eggs: 4-5; greenish blue with brown markings

Incubation: 12-13 days; female incubates

Fledging: 13-14 days; female and male feed young

Migration: irruptive; moves around in search of food

Food: seeds, insects, fruit; comes to seed feeders

Compare: Redder than the orange red of male House Finch (pg. 247), with a clear breast. Male House Finch has a brown cap unlike male Purple Finch's red cap. Male Red Crossbill (pg. 251) has a unique crossed bill.

Stan's Notes: A year-round resident in over half of New York. More commonly seen during migration in the rest of the state. In some parts of New York, often seen only in winter when flocks of Purple Finches leave their northern homes and move around searching for food. Visits seed feeders with House Finches, making it difficult to tell them apart. Eats mainly seeds. Prefers open woods or woodland edges. Travels in flocks of up to 50 birds. Has a rich loud song, with a distinctive "tic" note made only in flight. Not a purple color, Latin species name *purpureus* means "crimson" or other reddish color.

female pg. 283

male

YEAR-ROUND
WINTER

Red Crossbill
Loxia curvirostra

Size: 6½" (16 cm)

Male: Sparrow-sized bird, dirty red to orange with a bright red crown and rump. Dark brown wings. Short dark brown tail. Long, pointed crossed bill.

Female: pale yellow chest, light gray throat patch, a crossed bill, dark brown wings and tail

Juvenile: streaked with tinges of yellow, bill gradually crosses about 2 weeks after fledging

Nest: cup; female builds; 1 brood per year

Eggs: 3-4; bluish white with brown markings

Incubation: 14-18 days; female incubates

Fledging: 16-20 days; female and male feed young

Migration: irruptive; moves around the state in search of food, will wander as far south as Mexico

Food: seeds, leaf buds; comes to seed feeders

Compare: Larger than male House Finch (pg. 247). Similar shape, size and color as male Purple Finch (pg. 249). Look for the Red Crossbill's unique crossed bill.

Stan's Notes: The long crossed bill is adapted for extracting seeds from pine and spruce cones, its favorite food. Often dangles upside down like a parrot to reach cones. Also seen on the ground where it eats grit, which helps digest food. Plumage can be highly variable among individuals. Nests in coniferous forests. Red Crossbills from farther north move into New York in winter, searching for food, swelling resident populations. This irruptive behavior makes them more common in some winters and scarce in others.

 CD 2, TRACK 50

female
pg. 285

male

Scarlet Tanager
Piranga olivacea

SUMMER

Size: 7" (18 cm)

Male: Bright scarlet red bird with jet black wings and tail. Ivory bill and dark eyes.

Female: drab greenish yellow bird with olive wings and tail, whitish wing linings, dark eyes

Juvenile: same as female

Nest: cup; female builds; 1 brood per year

Eggs: 4-5; blue green with brown markings

Incubation: 13-14 days; female incubates

Fledging: 9-11 days; female and male feed young

Migration: complete, to Central and South America

Food: insects, fruit

Compare: Male Northern Cardinal (pg. 255) has a black mask and red bill and lacks the black wings of male Scarlet Tanager.

Stan's Notes: This is a tropical-looking bird that prefers mature, unbroken woodlands, where it hunts for insects high in the tops of trees. Requires at least 4 acres (1.5 ha) for nesting; prefers 8 acres (3 ha). It arrives late in spring and leaves early in fall. Male sheds (molts) its bright red plumage in the fall, appearing more like the female. Scarlet Tanagers are included in some 240 tanager species in the world. Nearly all are brightly colored and live in the tropics. The common name "Tanager" comes from a South American Tupi Indian word meaning "any small, brightly colored bird."

female pg. 123

male

juvenile

Northern Cardinal
Cardinalis cardinalis

Size: 8-9" (20-22.5 cm)

Male: All-red bird with a black mask that extends from the face down to the chin and throat. Large red bill and crest.

Female: buff brown with tinges of red on crest and wings, same black mask and red bill

Juvenile: same as female, but with a blackish gray bill

Nest: cup; female builds; 2-3 broods per year

Eggs: 3-4; bluish white with brown markings

Incubation: 12-13 days; female and male incubate

Fledging: 9-10 days; female and male feed young

Migration: non-migrator

Food: seeds, insects, fruit; comes to seed feeders

Compare: The male Red Crossbill (pg. 251) has dark brown wings and a thinner crossed bill. The male Scarlet Tanager (pg. 253) has black wings and tail. Look for the male Cardinal's black mask, large crest and red bill.

Stan's Notes: A familiar backyard bird. Look for the male feeding female during courtship. Male feeds young of the first brood by himself while female builds second nest. The name comes from the Latin word *cardinalis*, which means "important." Very territorial in spring, it will fight its own reflection in a window. Non-territorial during winter, gathering in small flocks of up to 20 birds. Both the male and female sing and can be heard anytime of year. Listen for its "whata-cheer-cheer-cheer" territorial call in the spring.

male

female pg. 203

Pine Grosbeak
Pinicola enucleator

Size: 9" (22.5 cm)

Male: Plump rosy red and gray winter finch with a long dark tail. Smattering of gray on dark wings. Two white wing bars. Short, stubby, pointed dark bill.

Female: mostly gray with dark wings and tail, head and rump tinged dull yellow

Juvenile: male has a touch of red on head and rump, female is similar to adult female

Nest: cup; female builds; 1 brood per year

Eggs: 4-5; bluish green without markings

Incubation: 13-15 days; female incubates

Fledging: 13-20 days; female and male feed young

Migration: irruptive; moves around to find food

Food: seeds, fruit, insects; will come to feeders

Compare: Much larger than the male Purple Finch (pg. 249) and male House Finch (pg. 247).

Stan's Notes: This winter finch is common in New York in some years and not so common in others. A very tame and approachable bird. Often seen along roads or on the ground, eating tiny grains of sand and dirt to aid digestion. A seed eater that favors coniferous forests, rarely moving out of coniferous regions during summer. Frequently seen bathing in fluffy snow. Flies with a typical finch-like undulating pattern while it calls a soft whistle. During breeding season, the male and female develop a pouch in the bottom of the mouth (buccal pouch) to transport seeds to young.

in flight

male pg. 237

female

Common Merganser

Mergus merganser

Size: 25" (63 cm)

Female: A long, thin, duck-like bird with a rust red head and ragged "hair" on the back of head. Gray body with white chest and chin. Long, pointed orange bill.

Male: same size and shape as the female, but with a green head, black back, white sides, chest and neck and long, pointed orange bill

Juvenile: same as female

Nest: cavity; female lines old woodpecker cavity; 1 brood per year

Eggs: 9-11; ivory without markings

Incubation: 28-33 days; female incubates

Fledging: 70-80 days; female feeds young

Migration: complete, to New York, southern states, Mexico and Central America

Food: small fish, aquatic insects

Compare: Hard to confuse with other birds. Look for ragged "hair" on back of a red head, a long, pointed orange bill, white chest and chin.

Stan's Notes: The merganser is a shallow water diver that feeds on small fish in 10-15 feet (3-4.5 m) of water. Bill has a fine serrated-like edge to help catch slippery fish. Females often lay eggs in other merganser nests (egg dumping), resulting in broods of up to 15 young per mother. Male leaves female when she starts to incubate her eggs. Orphans are accepted by other merganser mothers with young. Can be seen on just about any open water during winter.

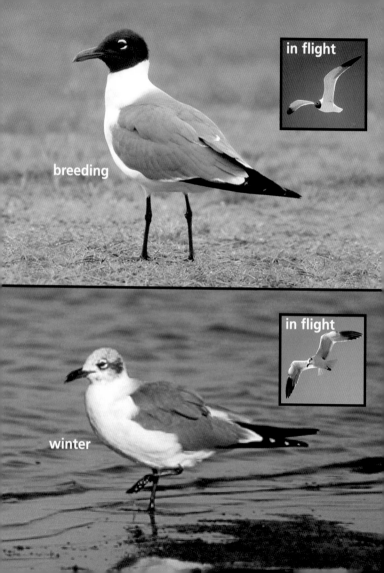

in flight

breeding

in flight

winter

Laughing Gull
Larus atricilla

Size: 16-17" (40-43 cm); up to 3⅕-foot wingspan

Male: Breeding adult has a black head "hood" and white neck, chest and belly. Slate gray back and wings with black wing tips. Orange bill. Incomplete white eye-ring. Winter plumage lacks the "hood" and has a black bill.

Female: same as male

Juvenile: brown throughout, gray sides, lacking the black head and white chest, has a gray bill

Nest: ground; male and female construct; 1 brood per year

Eggs: 2-4; olive with brown markings

Incubation: 18-20 days; female and male incubate

Fledging: 30-35 days; male and female feed young

Migration: partial to non-migrator in New York

Food: fish, insects, aquatic insects

Compare: Smaller than the Ring-billed Gull (pg. 263) and Herring Gull (pg. 265). Look for the black head "hood" and slate gray back and wings of the Laughing Gull.

Stan's Notes: This is a three-year gull that starts out mostly brown and gray. The second year it resembles adults, but lacks a complete black head "hood." Breeding plumage in the third year. Male tosses its head back and calls to attract a mate. Nests in marshes in large colonies. Nest is a scrape on the ground lined with grass, sticks and rocks. Adults regurgitate food to feed young.

in flight

breeding

juvenile

winter

Ring-billed Gull
Larus delawarensis

YEAR-ROUND
MIGRATION

Size: 19" (48 cm); up to 4-foot wingspan

Male: A white bird with gray wings, black wing tips spotted with white, and a white tail, as seen in flight. Yellow bill with a black ring near tip. Yellowish legs and feet. Winter or non-breeding adult has a speckled brown back of head and nape of neck.

Female: same as male

Juvenile: mostly gray version of winter adult, has a dark band at end of tail

Nest: ground; female and male construct; 1 brood per year

Eggs: 2-4; off-white with brown markings

Incubation: 20-21 days; female and male incubate

Fledging: 20-40 days; female and male feed young

Migration: partial to non-migrator in New York

Food: insects, fish; scavenges for food

Compare: Laughing Gull (pg. 261) has a black head "hood." The Herring Gull (pg. 265) has an orange-red mark on its lower bill and pink legs. Great Black-backed Gull (pg. 53) has a black back and orange spot on lower bill.

Stan's Notes: A common gull of garbage dumps and parking lots. Expanding its range and staying farther north longer in winter due to successful scavenging in cities. A three-year gull with different plumages in its first three autumns. Attains ring on bill after its first winter and adult plumage in the third year. Defends a small area around nest.

breeding

winter

juvenile

Herring Gull
Larus argentatus

YEAR-ROUND MIGRATION

Size: 23-26" (58-66 cm); up to 5-foot wingspan

Male: Snow-white bird with slate gray wings and black wing tips with tiny white spots. Bill is yellow with an orange-red spot near the tip of lower bill. Pinkish legs. Winter plumage head and neck are dirty gray to brown.

Female: same as male

Juvenile: uniformly mottled brown to gray, black bill

Nest: ground; female and male construct; 1 brood per year

Eggs: 2-3; olive with brown markings

Incubation: 24-28 days; female and male incubate

Fledging: 35-36 days; female and male feed young

Migration: partial to non-migrator in New York

Food: fish, insects, clams, eggs, baby birds

Compare: Larger than the Ring-billed Gull (pg. 263), which has yellowish legs, a black ring near the tip of its bill and lacks the orange-red spot on its lower mandible.

Stan's Notes: Common gull of large lakes. An opportunistic bird, scavenging for food from dumpsters, but will also take other birds' eggs and young right from nest. Often drops clams and other shellfish from heights to break shells and get to the soft interior. Nests in colonies, returning to same site year after year. Lines ground nest with grasses and seaweed. Takes about four years for juveniles to obtain adult plumage. Adults molt to a dirty gray in the winter, and look similar to juveniles.

in flight

Great Egret
Ardea alba

MIGRATION SUMMER

Size: 38" (96 cm); up to 4½-foot wingspan

Male: Tall, thin, elegant all-white bird with a long, pointed yellow bill. Black stilt-like legs and black feet.

Female: same as male

Juvenile: same as adult

Nest: platform; male and female build; 1 brood per year

Eggs: 2-3; light blue without markings

Incubation: 23-26 days; female and male incubate

Fledging: 43-49 days; female and male feed young

Migration: complete, to southern states, Mexico and Central America

Food: fish, aquatic insects, frogs, crayfish

Compare: Great Blue Heron (pg. 227) has a similar shape, but is larger in size and is not white.

Stan's Notes: A tall and stately bird, the Great Egret slowly stalks shallow wetlands looking for small fish to spear with its long sharp bill. Nests in colonies of up to 100 individuals. Now protected, it was hunted to near extinction in the 1800s and early 1900s for its long white plumage. The common name "Egret" came from the French word *aigrette*, which means "ornamental tufts of plumes." The plumes grow near the tail during breeding season.

Mute Swan
Cygnus olor

Size: 60" (152 cm); up to 7-foot wingspan

Male: Completely white bird. Holds its neck in an S shape with bill pointed toward the surface of water. Large orange bill with a prominent black knob at the base.

Female: same as male

Juvenile: brown-to-gray bird, gray bill with a black base, bill lacks a prominent knob

Nest: ground; female and male construct; 1 brood per year

Eggs: 4-8; light gray without markings

Incubation: 35-40 days; female and male incubate

Fledging: 115-150 days; female and male feed young

Migration: non-migrator to partial; will move to areas with open water during winter

Food: aquatic insects and plants

Compare: Hard to confuse with other birds. Look for a long-necked white bird with a large orange bill and prominent black knob on the face.

Stan's Notes: Usually silent, not mute. Makes a variety of sounds including hisses, barks and snorts when agitated. An introduced species, frequently in lakes, parks, zoos, golf courses and private property, now found in the wild. Often swims with wings arched over its back. Neck is always held in an S shape. Uses neck to reach plants on lake or pond bottom. Forms a long-term pair bond. Pairs defend large territories, driving off any other large birds including native swans and geese. Some states work to reduce the number of Mute Swans because of the fear of competition with native species.

MUTE (not on CD)

male pg. 241

female

American Redstart

Setophaga ruticilla

SUMMER

Size: 5" (13 cm)

Female: Olive brown with yellow patches on sides, wings and tail. White belly.

Male: small, striking black bird with contrasting patches of orange on sides, wings and tail, white belly

Juvenile: same as female, the juvenile male is tinged orange in the first year

Nest: cup; female builds; 1 brood per year

Eggs: 3-5; off-white with brown markings

Incubation: 12 days; female incubates

Fledging: 9 days; female and male feed young

Migration: complete, to Mexico, Central America and South America

Food: insects, seeds, berries rarely

Compare: Similar to female Yellow-rumped Warbler (pg. 185), but lacks the Yellow-rumped's yellow patch on rump.

Stan's Notes: This is a common and widespread breeding warbler in New York. Prefers large unbroken tracts of forest. Appears to be hyperactive when feeding, hovering and darting back and forth to glean insects from leaves. Often droops its wings and fans tail just before launching out to catch an insect. Look for the male's flashing black and orange colors high up in trees.

winter male

male

female

American Goldfinch
Carduelis tristis

Size: 5" (13 cm)

Male: A perky yellow bird with a black patch on forehead. Black tail with conspicuous white rump. Black wings with white wing bars. No marking on the chest. Dramatic change in color during winter, similar to female.

Female: dull olive yellow without a black forehead, with brown wings and a white rump

Juvenile: same as female

Nest: cup; female builds; 1 brood per year

Eggs: 4-6; pale blue without markings

Incubation: 10-12 days; female incubates

Fledging: 11-17 days; female and male feed young

Migration: partial migrator; small flocks of up to 20 birds move around North America, small percentage in New York will not migrate

Food: seeds, insects; will come to seed feeders

Compare: The male Yellow Warbler (pg. 279) is yellow with orange streaks on the chest. Pine Siskin (pg. 85) has a streaked chest and belly and yellow wing bars. Both female House Finch (pg. 81) and Purple Finch (pg. 95) have heavily streaked chests.

Stan's Notes: Often in open fields, scrubby areas and woodlands. A feeder bird that enjoys Nyjer thistle. Late summer nester, using silky down from wild thistle for its nest. Appears roller-coaster-like in flight. Twitters during flight. Almost always in small flocks. Moves only far enough south to find food. Frequently called Wild Canary.

Common Yellowthroat
Geothlypis trichas

SUMMER

Size: 5" (13 cm)

Male: Olive brown bird with bright yellow throat and breast, a white belly and a distinctive black mask outlined in white. A long, thin, pointed black bill.

Female: similar to male, lacks the black mask

Juvenile: same as female

Nest: cup; female builds; 2 broods per year

Eggs: 3-5; white with brown markings

Incubation: 11-12 days; female incubates

Fledging: 10-11 days; female and male feed young

Migration: complete, to southern states, Mexico and Central America

Food: insects

Compare: Found in a similar habitat as the American Goldfinch (pg. 273), but lacks the male's black forehead and wings. The male Yellow Warbler (pg. 279) has fine orange streaks on the breast and lacks male Yellowthroat's mask. Yellow-rumped Warbler (pg. 185) has only spots of yellow compared with the Yellowthroat's bright yellow breast.

Stan's Notes: A common warbler of open fields and marshes. Has a cheerful, well-known song, "witchity-witchity-witchity-witchity." The male performs a curious courtship display, bouncing in and out of tall grass while uttering an unusual song. The young remain dependent upon the parents longer than most warblers. A frequent cowbird host.

Magnolia Warbler
Dendroica magnolia

MIGRATION
SUMMER

Size: 5" (13 cm)

Male: Yellow and black warbler with a gray crown and white eyebrows. Heavy black streaks on a yellow chest and belly. White wing patch. Yellow rump. Obvious white patches on tail.

Female: similar to male, lacks black on the face, has 2 white wing bars

Juvenile: same as female

Nest: cup; female and male construct; 1 brood per year

Eggs: 3-5; white with brown markings

Incubation: 11-13 days; female incubates

Fledging: 8-10 days; female and male feed young

Migration: complete, to Central America

Food: insects

Compare: More yellow than Yellow-rumped Warbler (pg. 185). Yellow Warbler (pg. 279) lacks black on the face and a black back. Palm Warbler (pg. 281) has a chestnut cap and thin chestnut streaks on the sides of breast.

Stan's Notes: Common in the state during spring migration. Nests in parts of New York, other northern states and Canada. Has stable populations because of its ability to adapt to second growth forest. Look for it low in trees, where it feeds on insects. Frequently fans tail while picking insects from undersides of leaves. Male usually feeds higher up in trees than the female. Named by chance when ornithologist Alexander Wilson spotted the bird in a magnolia tree.

male

female

Yellow Warbler
Dendroica petechia

Size: 5" (13 cm)

Male: Yellow warbler with orange streaks on the chest and belly. Long, pointed dark bill.

Female: same as male, but lacking orange streaking

Juvenile: similar to female, only much duller

Nest: cup; female builds; 1 brood per year

Eggs: 4-5; white with brown markings

Incubation: 11-12 days; female incubates

Fledging: 10-12 days; female and male feed young

Migration: complete, to southern states, Mexico and Central and South America

Food: insects

Compare: Yellow-rumped Warbler (pg. 185) has only spots of yellow unlike the orange streaking on the chest of male Yellow Warbler. Male American Goldfinch (pg. 273) has a black forehead and wings. The female Yellow Warbler is similar to the female Goldfinch (pg. 273), but lacks white wing bars.

Stan's Notes: A widespread, common summer warbler in the state. Seen in gardens and shrubby areas near water. It is a prolific insect eater, gleaning small caterpillars and other insects from tree leaves. Male is often seen higher up in trees than the female. Female is less conspicuous. Starts to migrate south in July and is gone by August. Males arrive 1-2 weeks before females to claim territories. Migrates at night in mixed flocks of warblers. Rests and feeds during the day.

Palm Warbler
Dendroica palmarum

MIGRATION

Size: 5½" (14 cm)

Male: Distinctive yellow eyebrows. Yellow throat, belly and undertail. Obvious chestnut cap. Thin chestnut streaks on the sides of breast. Dark line across dark eyes.

Female: same as male

Juvenile: same as adult, but duller and brown

Nest: cup; female builds; 1-2 broods per year

Eggs: 4-5; white with brown markings

Incubation: 11-12 days; female incubates

Fledging: 12-13 days; female and male feed young

Migration: complete, to southeastern coastal states, the West Indies and Central America

Food: insects, fruit

Compare: The Yellow-rumped Warbler (pg. 185) has a similar size, but lacks a yellow throat and belly. Yellow Warbler (pg. 279) is slightly smaller and lacks a chestnut cap. Look for the yellow eyebrows and chestnut cap of the Palm Warbler.

Stan's Notes: One of the most common and abundant warblers, frequently seen in backyard woodlands during migration. After the Yellow-rumped Warbler, it is often the second warbler species seen during spring migration. Watch it wag or bob its tail while gleaning insects from leaves and flowers of trees. One of the few warblers to feed on the ground. Hops rather than walks. Nests at the edges of northern spruce bogs. Recognizes and destroys cowbird eggs, burying them with its nest, which it builds on top of the cowbird nest.

female

male pg. 251

Scarlet Tanager
Piranga olivacea

SUMMER

Size: 7" (18 cm)

Female: Drab greenish yellow bird with olive wings and tail. Whitish wing linings. Dark eyes.

Male: bright scarlet red bird with jet black wings and tail, ivory bill and dark eyes

Juvenile: same as female

Nest: cup; female builds; 1 brood per year

Eggs: 4-5; blue green with brown markings

Incubation: 13-14 days; female incubates

Fledging: 9-11 days; female and male feed young

Migration: complete, to Central and South America

Food: insects, fruit

Compare: The female Baltimore Oriole (pg. 287) has gray brown wings and white wing bars. Female American Goldfinch (pg. 273) is smaller and has white wing bars.

Stan's Notes: This is a tropical-looking bird that prefers mature, unbroken woodlands, where it hunts for insects high in the tops of trees. Requires at least 4 acres (1.5 ha) for nesting; prefers 8 acres (3 ha). It arrives late in spring and leaves early in fall. Male sheds (molts) its bright red plumage in the fall, appearing more like the female. Scarlet Tanagers are included in some 240 tanager species in the world. Nearly all are brightly colored and live in the tropics. The common name "Tanager" comes from a South American Tupi Indian word meaning "any small, brightly colored bird."

male pg. 243

female

Baltimore Oriole
Icterus galbula

SUMMER

Size: 7-8" (18-20 cm)

Female: A pale yellow bird with orange tones, gray brown wings, white wing bars, a gray bill and dark eyes.

Male: bright flaming orange bird with black head and black extending down nape of neck onto the back, black wings with white and orange wing bars, an orange tail with black streaks, gray bill and dark eyes

Juvenile: same as female

Nest: pendulous; female builds; 1 brood per year

Eggs: 4-5; bluish with brown markings

Incubation: 12-14 days; female incubates

Fledging: 12-14 days; female and male feed young

Migration: complete, to Mexico, Central America and South America

Food: insects, fruit, nectar; comes to orange half and nectar feeders

Compare: Very similar to the female Orchard Oriole (pg. 289), which lacks orange tones and has less pronounced wing bars.

Stan's Notes: A fantastic songster, this bird usually is heard before seen. Easily attracted to a feeder offering grape jelly, orange halves or sugar water (nectar). Parents bring young to feeders. Sits in tops of trees feeding on caterpillars. Female builds a sock-like nest at the outermost branches of tall trees. Often returns to the same area year after year. Some of the last birds to arrive in spring (May) and first to leave in fall (September).

male
pg. 245

female

SUMMER

Orchard Oriole
Icterus spurius

Size: 7-8" (18-20 cm)

Female: An olive green bird with a dull yellow belly. Two white wing bars on dark gray wings. Long, thin black bill with a small gray mark on lower mandible (jaw).

Male: dull orange with a black head, chin, upper back, wings and tail, single white wing bars

Juvenile: same as female, black bib on first-year male

Nest: pendulous; female builds; 1 brood per year

Eggs: 3-5; pale blue to white, brown markings

Incubation: 11-12 days; female and male incubate

Fledging: 11-14 days; female and male feed young

Migration: complete, to Mexico, Central America and northern South America

Food: insects, fruit; comes to fruit/nectar feeders

Compare: Female Baltimore Oriole (pg. 287) is similar, but has orange tones and more pronounced wing bars. Female Scarlet Tanager (pg. 285) has olive wings.

Stan's Notes: Prefers orchards or open woods, hence its common name. Eats insects until wild fruit starts to ripen. One of the last birds to arrive in spring and one of the first to leave in fall. Spends 3-4 months in New York. Often migrates with the more abundant Baltimore Oriole. Frequently nests alone, but sometimes nests in small colonies. Parents bring young to jelly and orange half feeders just after fledging. Many people think the orioles have left during summer, but the birds are concentrating on finding insects to feed their young. Common in the southern half of New York.

 CD 2, TRACK 49

male

juvenile

female

Evening Grosbeak
Coccothraustes vespertinus

YEAR-ROUND
WINTER

Size: 8" (20 cm)

Male: A striking bird with a stocky body, a large ivory-to-greenish bill and bright yellow eyebrows. Dirty yellow head, yellow rump and belly and black-and-white wings and tail.

Female: similar to male, with softer colors and a gray head and throat

Juvenile: similar to female, with a brown bill

Nest: cup; female builds; 1 brood per year

Eggs: 3-4; blue with brown markings

Incubation: 12-14 days; female incubates

Fledging: 13-14 days; female and male feed young

Migration: irruptive; moves around the state in winter to find food

Food: seeds, insects, fruit; comes to seed feeders

Compare: Larger than its close relative, the Goldfinch (pg. 273). The female Evening Grosbeak is slightly smaller than female Pine Grosbeak (pg. 203) and has a gray head. Look for the male Evening Grosbeak's dark head, bright yellow eyebrows and large thick bill.

Stan's Notes: One of the largest finches. Characteristic undulating finch-like flight. An unusually large bill for cracking seeds, its main food source. Often seen on gravel roads eating gravel, from which it gets minerals, salt and grit to grind the seeds it eats. Sheds the outer layer of its bill in spring, exposing a blue green bill. Moves in large flocks in winter, searching for food, often coming to feeders. More numerous in some years than others.

Eastern Meadowlark
Sturnella magna

Size: 9" (22.5 cm)

Male: Robin-shaped bird with a yellow breast and belly, brown back and prominent black V-shaped necklace. White outer tail feathers.

Female: same as male

Juvenile: same as adult

Nest: cup, on the ground in dense cover; female builds; 2 broods per year

Eggs: 3-5; white with brown markings

Incubation: 13-15 days; female incubates

Fledging: 11-12 days; female and male feed young

Migration: partial to non-migrator in New York

Food: insects, seeds

Compare: Horned Lark (pg. 113) is smaller and lacks a yellow breast and belly. Look for a black V mark on the breast of the Meadowlark.

Stan's Notes: A bird of open grassy country. Named "Meadowlark" because it's a bird of meadows and sings like the larks of Europe. Best known for its wonderful song—a flute-like, clear whistle. Often seen perching on fence posts, it will quickly dive into tall grass if approached. Conspicuous white markings on each side of its tail, most often seen when flying away. Nest is sometimes domed with dried grass. Not a member of the lark family, it actually belongs to the blackbird family and is related to grackles and orioles.

HELPFUL RESOURCES

Birder's Bug Book, The. Waldbauer, Gilbert. Cambridge: Harvard University Press, 1998.

Birder's Dictionary. Cox, Randall T. Helena, MT: Falcon Press Publishing, 1996.

Birder's Handbook, The. Ehrlich, Paul R., David S. Dobkin and Darryl Wheye. New York: Simon and Schuster, 1988.

Birds Do It, Too: The Amazing Sex Life of Birds. Harrison, Kit and George H. Harrison. Minocqua, WI: Willow Creek Press, 1997.

Birds of Forest, Yard, and Thicket. Eastman, John. Mechanicsburg, PA: Stackpole Books, 1997.

Birds of North America. Kaufman, Kenn. New York: Houghton Mifflin, 2000.

Blackbirds of the Americas. Orians, Gordon H. Seattle: University of Washington Press, 1985.

Bull's Birds of New York State. Levine, Emanuel. Ithaca: Comstock Publishing Associates, 1998.

Cardinal, The. Osborne, June. Austin: University of Texas Press, 1995.

Dictionary of American Bird Names, The. Choate, Ernest A. Boston: Harvard Common Press, 1985.

Dictionary of Birds of the United States. Holloway, Joel E. Portland, OR: Timber Press, 2003.

Everything You Never Learned About Birds. Rupp, Rebecca. Pownal, VT: Storey Publishing, 1997.

Field Guide to the Birds, A: A Completely New Guide to All the Birds of Eastern and Central North America. Peterson, Roger Tory and Virginia Marie Peterson. Boston: Houghton Mifflin, 1998.

Field Guide to the Birds of North America: Third Edition. Washington, DC: National Geographic Society, 1999.

Field Guide to Warblers of North America, A. Dunn, Jon and Kimball Garrett. Boston: Houghton Mifflin, 1997.

Folklore of Birds. Martin, Laura C. Old Saybrook, CT: Globe Pequot Press, 1996.

Guide to Bird Behavior, A: Vol I, II, III. Stokes, Donald and Lillian Stokes. Boston: Little, Brown and Company, 1989.

How Birds Migrate. Kerlinger, Paul. Mechanicsburg, PA: Stackpole Books, 1995.

Lives of Birds, The: Birds of the World and Their Behavior. Short, Lester L. Collingdale, PA: DIANE Publishing, 2000.

Living on the Wind. Weidensaul, Scott. New York: North Point Press, 2000.

National Audubon Society: North American Birdfeeder Handbook. Burton, Robert. New York: Dorling Kindersley Publishing, 1995.

National Audubon Society: The Sibley Guide to Bird Life and Behavior. Edited by David Allen Sibley, Chris Elphick and John B. Dunning, Jr. New York: Alfred A. Knopf, 2001.

National Audubon Society: The Sibley Guide to Birds. Sibley, David Allen. New York: Alfred A. Knopf, 2000.

Photographic Guide to North American Raptors, A. Wheeler, Brian K. and William S. Clark. New York: Academic Press, 1999.

Raptors of Eastern North America: The Wheeler Guides. Wheeler, Brian K. Princeton, NJ: Princeton University Press, 2003.

Secret Lives of Birds, The. Gingras, Pierre. Toronto: Key Porter Books, 1997.

Secrets of the Nest. Dunning, Joan. Boston: Houghton Mifflin, 1994.

Sparrows and Buntings: A Guide to the Sparrows and Buntings of North America and the World. Byers, Clive, Jon Curson and Urban Olsson. New York: Houghton Mifflin, 1995.

Stokes Bluebird Book: The Complete Guide to Attracting Bluebirds. Stokes, Donald and Lillian Stokes. Boston: Little, Brown and Company, 1991.

Stokes Field Guide to Birds: Eastern Region. Stokes, Donald and Lillian Stokes. Boston: Little, Brown and Company, 1996.

Stokes Purple Martin Book. Stokes, Donald and Lillian Stokes. Boston: Little, Brown and Company, 1997.

New York Birding Hotlines

To report unusual bird sightings or possibly hear recordings of where birds have been seen, you can often call pre-recorded hotlines detailing such information. Since these hotlines are usually staffed by volunteers, and phone numbers and even the organizations that host them often change, the phone numbers are not listed here. To obtain the numbers, go to your favorite internet search engine, type in something like "rare bird alert hotline New York" and follow the links provided.

Web Pages

The internet is a valuable place to learn more about birds. You may find birding on the net a fun way to discover additional information or to spend a long winter night. These web sites will assist you in your pursuit of birds. If a web address doesn't work (they often change a bit), just enter the name of the group into a search engine to track down the new web address.

Site	Address
Audubon New York	http://ny.audubon.org
New York State Ornithological Association	www.nybirds.org
American Birding Association	www.americanbirding.org
Cornell Lab of Ornithology	www.birds.cornell.edu
Author Stan Tekiela's home page	www.naturesmart.com

CHECKLIST/INDEX BY SPECIES

Use the boxes to check the birds you've seen.

"CD Track" refers to the *Birds of New York Audio CDs* by Stan Tekiela.

"CD Track" refers to the *Birds of New York Audio CDs* by Stan Tekiela.

"CD Track" refers to the *Birds of New York Audio CDs* by Stan Tekiela.

"CD Track" refers to the *Birds of New York Audio CDs* by Stan Tekiela.

"CD Track" refers to the *Birds of New York Audio CDs* by Stan Tekiela.

ABOUT THE AUTHOR

Naturalist, wildlife photographer and writer Stan Tekiela is the originator of the popular state-specific field guide series that includes *Trees of New York Field Guide*. For over two decades, Stan has authored more than 100 field guides, nature appreciation books and wildlife audio CDs for nearly every state in the nation, presenting many species of birds, mammals, reptiles and amphibians, trees, wildflowers and cacti. Holding a Bachelor of Science degree in Natural History from the University of Minnesota and as an active professional naturalist for more than 20 years, Stan studies and photographs wildlife throughout the United States and has received various national and regional awards for his books and photographs. Also a well-known columnist and radio personality, his syndicated column appears in more than 20 newspapers and his wildlife programs are broadcast on a number of Midwest radio stations. He is a member of the North American Nature Photography Association and Canon Professional Services. Stan resides in Victoria, Minnesota, with his wife, Katherine, and daughter, Abigail. He can be contacted via his web page at www.naturesmart.com.

An easy-to-use field guide...

- **Efficient:** 120 common species—only New York birds!
- **Easy:** See a yellow bird? Find it in the book's yellow section
- **Helpful:** Compare feature to distinguish between look-alikes
- **Engaging:** Stan's Notes provide naturalist tidbits and facts
- **Stunning:** Crisp, incomparable full-page photographs

...with a great design

The CD icon on each page directs you to the track on the *Birds of New York Audio CDs* (sold separately), so you can immediately hear the songs and calls of each bird

About the Author

Stan Tekiela is a naturalist, wildlife photographer and the originator of many popular state-specific field guides. He has authored more than 100 field guides, nature books and audio CDs, presenting many species of birds, mammals, reptiles and amphibians, trees, wildflowers and cacti.

COLLECT ALL THE NEW YORK FIELD GUIDES

$13.95

Adventure Publications, Inc.
820 Cleveland Street South
Cambridge, MN 55008
1-800-678-7006
www.adventurepublications.net
ISBN: 978-1-59193-108-9

ISBN 1-59193-108-8

5 1 3 9 5

9 781591 931089

Red Crossbill
Loxia curvirostra

Size: 6½" (16 cm)

Female: A pale yellow-gray sparrow-sized bird with a pale yellow chest and light gray patch on the throat. Dark brown wings. Short dark brown tail. Long, pointed crossed bill.

Male: dirty red to orange with a bright red crown and rump, dark brown wings, a short dark brown tail and a crossed bill

Juvenile: streaked with tinges of yellow, bill gradually crosses about 2 weeks after fledging

Nest: cup; female builds; 1 brood per year

Eggs: 3-4; bluish white with brown markings

Incubation: 14-18 days; female incubates

Fledging: 16-20 days; female and male feed young

Migration: irruptive; moves around the state in search of food, will wander as far south as Mexico

Food: seeds, leaf buds; comes to seed feeders

Compare: The female American Goldfinch (pg. 273) is smaller. The female Purple Finch (pg. 95) has a similar shape and size. Look for the Red Crossbill's unique crossed bill.

Stan's Notes: The long crossed bill is adapted for extracting seeds from pine and spruce cones, its favorite food. Often dangles upside down like a parrot to reach cones. Also seen on the ground where it eats grit, which helps digest food. Plumage can be highly variable among individuals. Nests in coniferous forests. Red Crossbills from farther north move into New York in winter, swelling populations. More common in some winters and scarce in others.

female

male pg. 253